Illustrators of Books
for
Young People

by
Martha E. Ward
and
Dorothy A. Marquardt

The Scarecrow Press, Inc.
Metuchen, N.J.   1970

Contents

i

Preface

Illustrators of Books For Young People includes 370 biographies.
The format and factors for determining inclusion were based on
the authors' previous publications: Authors of Books For Young
People, c. 1964, and Authors of Books For Young People, First
Supplement, c. 1967. The following factors were used in
determining illustrators to be included:

(1)   This book has been based on biographical information
        compiled in the Children's Department of the Free Public
        Library, Quincy, Illinois. Any contemporary illustrator
        whose biography proved difficult to locate was given pref-
        erence for inclusion over a well-known illustrator whose
        biographical information was more readily available.

(2)   All recipients of the Caldecott (1938-1969) Medal have
        been included. This information was taken from the
        authors' publications mentioned above, and reference to
        this source is given following each entry. The Caldecott
        Medal is awarded "to the artist of the most distinguished
        American picture book for children."

The symbols which follow the biographies refer to volumes in
which additional illustrator information can be found.

Key to Symbols

ICB-1   Illustrators of Children's Books, 1744-1945.
          Bertha E. Mahony, Louise Payson Latimer,
          Beulah Folmsbee, compilers. (c. 1947)
          The Horn Book Inc. Boston

ICB-2   Illustrators of Children's Books, 1946-1956.
Ruth Hill Viguers, Marcia Dalphin, Bertha
Mahony Miller, compilers. (c. 1958) The
Horn Book. Boston

ICB-3   Illustrators of Children's Books, 1957-1966.
Lee Kingman, Joanna Foster, Ruth Giles
Lontoft, compilers. (c. 1968) The Horn
Book, Inc. Boston

We are grateful for our jobs as children's librarians in a
public library. Our work gives us the opportunity to see a
need, and a public library provides us with the resources to
fill it.

Martha E. Ward

Dorothy A. Marquardt

Illustrators of Books For Young People

ADAMS, Adrienne

Illustrator and teacher, born in Fort Smith, Arkansas.
She attended Stephens College at Columbia, Missouri,
graduated from the University of Missouri, and studied at
New York's American School of Design. She married
writer John Lonzo Anderson, and they have lived in
Hunterdon County, New Jersey. Miss Adams' illustrations of several fairy tales were selected as "Notable
Books" by the American Library Association. Juvenile
books which she illustrated include: Cabbage Moon, Wahl,
J., Holt, 1965; Candy Floss (A Junior Literary Guild
selection), Godden, R., Viking, 1960; In the Middle of
the Night, Fisher, A., Crowell, 1965.   ICB-2, ICB-3

AKINO, Fuku 1908-

Artist and teacher, born in Futamata, Tenryu City, Japan.
She studied at the Sizuoka Normal School and later attended private art classes in Tokyo and Kyoto. In addition
to drawing and painting, Miss Akino has been an elementary school teacher. She later became Assistant
Professor at the Municipal Art Academy in Kyoto. The
artist helped to organize the Shinseisaku Association in
1948. She has been the recipient of many honors including the highest award presented to a woman artist, the
Uemura Shoen Prize. Juvenile books which she has
illustrated include: The Cock and the Ghost Cat, Lifton,

5

B. , Atheneum, 1965; <u>The One-Legged Ghost</u>, Lifton, B. ,
Atheneum, 1968.   ICB-3

ALCORN, John 1935-
He was born in Corona, Long Island, New York. Mr.
Alcorn studied at Cooper Union. His work has won
awards from the Type Directors Club, the New York Art
Directors Club, the Society of Illustrators, and the
American Institute of Graphic Arts. He has lived with
his wife and four sons in Ossining, New York. His
books include: <u>La Fiesta</u>, Joslin, S. , Harcourt, 1967;
<u>La Petite Famille</u>, Joslin, S. , Harcourt, 1964.   ICB-3

ALEXANDER, Martha
She was born in Georgia. She has illustrated the picture
books of many leading authors. At one time she lived
in Hawaii; however, she later made her home in New
York City. Her work includes: <u>Mary Ann's Mud Day</u>,
Udry, J. , Harper, 1967; <u>What Is A Whispery Secret?</u>,
Hobart, L. , Parents' Magazine Press, 1968.

ALMQUIST, Don
After graduating from the Rhode Island School of Design
in 1951, he studied with Jose Guerrero. His career as
an artist has included magazine work, book illustration
for children, and advertising. Mr. Almquist has lived
in Bridgeport, Connecticut, but spent two years in Sweden
as Creative Director for a publishing firm. He has been
the recipient of many awards and honors. In 1956 he
won the silver medal from the Philadelphia Art Directors
Club. For boys and girls he illustrated <u>Spring Is Like</u>
<u>the Morning</u>, Craig, M. , Putnam, 1965.

ALOISE, Frank

Prior to his career in book illustration, he worked as an
artist in television.   Mr. Aloise studied in New York at
the Art Students League and the Workshop School of Art.
He has made his home in New York and has worked
with blind children at New York City's "Light House."
He has illustrated many books for boys and girls and
once said: "(children) are the truest, purest judges of
what an artist must do in order to successfully illustrate
a book for children." His work includes: Nathan Hale,
Voight, V., Putnam, 1965; Road to Raffydiddle, Merry-
man, M., Abingdon, 1966; Seashores and Seashore Creatures, Jackson, C., Putnam, 1964.

AMBRUS, Victor G.

He was born in Budapest, Hungary where he later studied
at the Academy of Fine Arts.   He won the 1964 Carnegie
Medal and several times was runner-up for the Kate
Greenaway Medal.   His wife has also been an artist, and
they have lived in Hampshire, England.   His books include: Henri's Hands for Pablo Picasso, Kay, H.
(pseud.), Abelard-Schuman, 1966; Private Beach (A
Junior Literary Guild selection), Parker, R., Duell,
1965.   ICB-3

ANDREWS, Benny

He has been a teacher of painting and drawing at New
York's New School for Social Research.   His work has
been exhibited at the Museum of African Art, the Brooklyn Museum, and the Museum of Modern Art.   His paintings have been included in the permanent collections of

the Norfolk and Chrysler Museums and the Joseph H.
Hirshhorn Collection.   He illustrated I Am the Darker
Brother, Adoff, A., ed., Macmillan, 1968.

ARNDT, Ursula
She was born in Germany.   Although she spent her childhood in her native land, she later came to America and
made her home in Brooklyn, New York.   Her illustrations
have not only appeared in books for boys and girls but
also in many magazines.   Her work includes: All the
Silver Pennies, Thompson, B., ed., Macmillan, 1967;
Troll Weather, Coatsworth, E., Macmillan, 1967.

ARNO, Enrico 1913-
Artist and teacher, born in Mannheim, Germany.   He
studied in Berlin at the State Academy.   Enrico Arno
came to the United States in 1947 and has lived in New
York on Long Island.   His hobby has been puppetry.   He
has been on the staff of Pratt Institute in Brooklyn and
Columbia University.   In addition to books, he has illustrated book jackets, magazines, and record covers.   For
children he illustrated Pomando, Craig, J., Norton,
1969.   ICB-2, ICB-3

ASMUSSEN, Des
He has made his home in Fredensborg, Denmark.   Mr.
Asmussen's pen-and-ink drawings have appeared in the
Saturday Evening Post.   Known throughout Europe for his
book illustrations, his work first appeared in an American
book for boys and girls in Leo Tolstoy's collection Ivan
the Fool, and Other Tales, Daniels, G., sel. and tr.

by, Macmillan, 1966.

AUSTIN, Phil

Watercolor artist, he studied at the University of Michigan and at the Academy of Art in Chicago.   Vincent
Price bought some of his paintings for the Sear's Collection.   His work has been exhibited at the Watercolor
Society of New York and at the Chicago Art Institute.
Mr. Austin and his family have lived in Waukegan, Illinois.   For young people he illustrated Colorado, Carpen-
ter, A. , Childrens Press, 1967.

AVISON, George   1885-

He was born in Norwalk, Connecticut and later studied
at the Chase School of Art in New York.   His drawings
were used to create the "Street of the Nineties" in the
1939 New York World's Fair.   In addition to illustrating
books, he has painted murals and designed houses.   The
artist has lived in Rowayton and New Canaan, Connecticut.   He illustrated: The Scrapper, Silliman, L. ,
Winston, 1946; White Captive of the Sioux, Miller, M. ,
Winston, 1953.   He also wrote and illustrated Uncle
Sam's Marines, How They Fight, Macmillan, 1944.

ICB-1, ICB-2

BALDRIDGE, Cyrus Le Roy   1889-

Cartoonist, illustrator, teacher.   Born in Alton, New
York, he later made his home in Santa Fe, New Mexico.
He received his art education at Frank Holme's School
of Illustration prior to graduating from the University of
Chicago.   At one time he served as President of the

National Association of Commercial Arts and of both the
University of Chicago Club and Artists Guild in New York.
Mr. Baldridge has been a lecturer and teacher of book
design in addition to illustrating books.   He traveled
throughout the Far East and visited the places mentioned
by Marco Polo in order to sketch authentic pictures for
Adventures and Discoveries of Marco Polo, Walsh, R.,
Random, 1953.   ICB-1, ICB-2

BALDWIN-FORD, Pamela
She spent her childhood in Torrington, Connecticut and
studied at the Paier School of Art in Hamden, Connecticut.
She later taught drawing and painting at Paier.   She
married artist and graphic designer Woodruff Ford and
has lived in New Haven, Connecticut.   For young people
she illustrated The Parsonage Parrot (A Junior Literary
Guild selection), Bothwell, J., Watts, 1969.

BARKER, Carol Minturn   1938-
Born in London, she studied at the School of Art,
Chelsea, London, Central School of Arts and Crafts,
London, and at the College of Art, Bournemouth, Hamp-
shire.   She also spent a year of training in graphic de-
sign in her father's studio.   Her first picture book in
color resulted from a 1960 visit to Greece.   Her work
includes: Achilles the Donkey, Bates, H., Watts, 1962;
I Wonder How, I Wonder Why, Fisher, A., Abelard-
Schuman, 1962.   ICB-3

BARRY, James E.
Artist, portrait painter, native New Yorker.   After grad-

uating from Brooklyn's Pratt Institute, he attended the
Art Career School in New York City. Mr. Barry served
in Army Intelligence during World War II. After the war
he devoted his time to painting portraits and book illustration which includes: The Story of Electricity and
Magnetism, Seeman, B. , Harvey, 1967; A Treasury of
Greek Mythology, Witting, A. , Harvey, 1966.

BASILEVSKY, Helen 1939-
She was born in Brussels, Belgium. She came to this
country in 1949 and lived in Sea Cliff, Long Island where
she has continued to live. After receiving a B. A. degree
from Pratt Institute in Brooklyn, Miss Basilevsky toured
Europe and the Middle East for six months. In 1963 she
served as an interpreter with the U. S. I. A. exhibit in
Russia. For children she illustrated Branislav The
Dragon (A Junior Literary Guild selection), Masey, M. ,
McKay, 1967.

BEGAY, Harrison
Illustrator and painter, born in Arizona on the Navajo
reservation at White Cone. Prior to World War II,
he attended Black Mountain College in North Carolina.
Mr. Begay has received many prizes for his work in
Indian art and was awarded the French Palme Academ-
ique medal for artistic achievement. His paintings have
been exhibited in art galleries and museums throughout
Europe and the United States. For boys and girls he
illustrated A Hogan For The Bluebird, Crowell, A. ,
Scribner, 1969.

BELTRÁN, Alberto   1923-

Artist, illustrator, engraver, born in Mexico City.   He
studied in Mexico at the Free School of Art and Public-
ity.   He was awarded the National Engraving Award in
1958 and placed first in the engraving section in the
1960 First Interamerican Painting and Engraving Bien-
nial held in Mexico City.   He has become known as
"the successor to the late Miguel Covarrubias" because
of his artistic abilities and deep understanding of Mexico's ancient Indian cultures.   For boys and girls he
illustrated Maya, Land Of The Turkey And The Deer,
VonHagen, V. , World, 1960.   ICB-3

BEMELMANS, Ludwig   1898-1962

Born in Meran (then part of Austria), the son of a Bel-
gian painter.   He came to the United States at the age
of sixteen.   Following his arrival in this country, he
worked in several New York hotels and studied painting.
His first children's book was Hansi (Viking, 1934).
Many of the incidents for his "Madeline" books were
provided during the author's stay in France.   In 1954
he was awarded the Caldecott Medal for his book Madeline's Rescue, Viking, 1953.   Juvenile titles include:
The High World, Harper, 1954; Parsley, Harper, 1955.
(Authors of Books For Young People-1964)
                              ICB-1, ICB-2, ICB-3

BENNETT, Susan

She was born in Minnesota and has made her home in
New York City.   Miss Bennett studied art in St. Olaf
College in Northfield, Minnesota.   She later attended

Bileck, Marvin 1920-

art and music classes at the International Summer School in Oslo, Norway. For boys and girls she illustrated In-Between Miya, Uchida, Y., Scribner, 1967.

BILECK, Marvin 1920-

He was born in Passaic, New Jersey and studied at Cooper Union in New York and at the London School of Architecture in England. His pencil and water color drawings in Rain Makes Applesauce (Scheer, J., Holiday, 1964) received recognition not only as one of the New York Times' "Ten Best Illustrated Children's Books" but also as runner-up for the Caldecott Medal in 1965. He later taught at the Philadelphia College of Art. His work includes: Nobody's Birthday, Colver, A., Knopf, 1961; Sugarplum, Johnston, J., Knopf, 1955.   ICB-2, ICB-3

BIRD, Alice

Artist-illustrator. Since members of her family were scientists, Alice Bird grew up learning to appreciate and to observe accurately the world of nature. As a talented craftsman, she combined her knowledge of botany and art to portray realism in her book illustrations. Origrial lithographs were used in the book Trees of the Countryside, McKenny, M., Knopf, 1942.

BJORKLUND, Lorence F.

Artist-illustrator, born and educated in St. Paul, Minnesota. He later studied at Pratt Institute in Brooklyn. He has worked both in the magazine and advertising field but has preferred illustrating books. He has been interested in American history and travel. At one time he

traveled by rowboat from St. Paul to New Orleans.
Lorence Bjorklund has made his home in Croton Falls,
New York.   Juvenile books which he has illustrated in-
clude: American Forts, Yesterday And Today, Grant,
B. , Dutton, 1965; Pontiac: Lion In The Forest, Hays,
W. , Houghton, 1965; Stars And Stripes, Freeman, M. ,
Random, 1964; Thornbush Jungle, Montgomery, R. ,
World, 1966.   ICB-2, ICB-3

BLAKE, Quentin 1932-
Born in Sidcup, Kent, England, he studied at Downing
College, Cambridge and in London at the University Institute of Education.   He also attended the Chelsea School
of Art.   In addition to books, his illustrations have appeared in Punch magazine.   Prior to being an art instructor at the Royal College of Art in the School of
Graphic Design, Quentin Blake had taught English at the
French Lycee in London.   His home has been in London
in South Kensington.   For boys and girls he illustrated:
Pun Fun, Rees, E. , Abelard-Schuman, 1965; The Wonderful Button, Hunter, E. , Abelard-Schuman, 1961.   ICB-3

BLEGVAD, Erik 1923-
He was born and grew up in Copenhagen, Denmark where
he later studied at the school of Arts and Crafts.   Mr.
Blegvad has worked in a Copenhagen advertising agency,
as a free-lance artist in London, and later became well-
known in the United States as a magazine and book illustrator.   He married painter Lenore Hochman and has
lived in Westport, Connecticut.   His work includes:
Having a Friend, Miles, B. , Knopf, 1959; Mr. Jensen

  & Cat, Blegvad, L., Harcourt, 1965.   ICB-2, ICB-3

BLOCH, Lucienne 1909-

Born in Geneva, Switzerland, she studied at the Ecole
des Beaux Arts in Paris and also in Florence and Berlin.
She married artist Stephen P. Dmitroff, and they have
painted murals in Grand Rapids, Michigan and San Jose,
California. Museums in the United States and Europe
have had in their collections both her lithographs and
glass sculpture. The recipient of many awards, Lucienne
Bloch has made her home in Mill Valley, California.
She illustrated Sandpipers, Hurd, E., Crowell, 1961.

                                         ICB-1, ICB-2

BLUST, Earl R.

Artist, painter, print maker. Born in Harrisburg, Pennsylvania, he graduated from the College of Art in Philadelphia. He has lived in Lemoyne, Pennyslvania where
he has been an art director for the Krone Art Service.
His work has been shown in private collections and in
many exhibits. For children he illustrated Action at
Paradise Marsh (A Junior Literary Guild selection), Wier,
E., Stackpole, 1968.

BOBRI, V. see BOBRITSKY, Vladimir

BOBRITSKY, Vladimir 1898-

V. Bobri is his pseudonym. This artist and musician
was born in Kharkov, Ukraine. He studied at the
Kharkov Imperial Art School. Vladimir Bobri has been
recognized as an authority on folk lore of different

countries and on gypsy music.   Before coming to America in 1921, he worked with archeologists in Turkey and
the Crimea and painted icons in Greece.   Mr. Bobri
operated a textile firm in the United States, painted
murals, and worked in advertising in addition to book
illustration.   He has also served as editor of Guitar Review magazine.   He has directed radio programs of
chamber music.   The artist has received several citations
from the Art Directors Club for advertising design and
numerous awards for book illustration.   His work can be
found in Icebergs, Gans, R. , Crowell, 1964.

ICB-2, ICB-3

BODECKER, Nils Mogens 1922-
N. M. Bodecker was born in Copenhagen, Denmark where
he later studied art at the School of Applied Arts.   He
came to the United States in 1952.   He has been an editorial assistant on an art magazine, and his illustrations
have appeared in newspapers and magazines.   Mr. Bodecker has also written poetry.   He illustrated: Magic
Or Not?, Eager, E. , Harcourt, 1959; Seven-Day Magic,
Eager, E. , Harcourt, 1962.   ICB-2, ICB-3

BOLDEN, Joseph
A well-known artist, Joseph Bolden has worked in both
advertising and book illustration.   He studied at the
Philadelphia Museum School of Industrial Art.   His work
has appeared in Jack and Jill and other magazines.   For
young people he illustrated The Purple Tide, Silliman,
L. , Winston, 1949.

BOLOGNESE, Donald Alan 1934-

Calligrapher, illustrator, born in New York City. He
studied at Cooper Union Art School. His work has not
only appeared in books but also in the magazine sections
of newspapers. Mr. Bolognese has taught calligraphy
at Pratt Institute in Brooklyn. Books which he has illustrated include: Apple Seeds & Soda Straws, Ritchie, J.,
Walck, 1965; More Beautiful Than Flowers, Lexau, J.,
Lippincott, 1966.   ICB-3

BONSALL, Crosby Barbara (Newell) 1921-

Born in New York City, she later made her home in
Hillsgrove, Pennsylvania. She studied at the New York
University School of Architecture and American School
of Design in New York City. Mrs. Bonsall has worked
in advertising, written books, and created doll characters.
Crosby Bonsall has also illustrated books for other
writers. Some of her books have appeared under the
name of Crosby Newell. She illustrated Go Away, Dog,
Nodset, J., Harper, 1963. Juvenile books which she
wrote and illustrated include: The Case Of The Dumb
Bells, Harper, 1966; Who's A Pest?, Harper, 1962.

                                                     ICB-3

BOOTH, Graham 1935-

British artist and teacher. He was born in London,
grew up in Canada, and has lived in Placentia, California. He attended the University of California at Los
Angeles and received his master's degree in fine arts
from the University of Southern California. Graham
Booth has been an art director, free-lance artist, and

Borja, Corinne   Robert

has managed an advertising agency. At one time he
served on the staff of the Vancouver School of Art but later
taught art at Fullerton Junior College. Juvenile books
which he illustrated include: Henry the Explorer (A
Junior Literary Guild selection), Taylor, M. , Atheneum,
1966; Sing, Sailor, Sing, Martin, P. , Golden Gate, 1966.

ICB-3

BORJA, Corinne   Robert
Husband-wife team who have lived in Chicago. Both
attended the Institute of Design and the American Academy
of Art. Corinne Borja has worked as a fashion illustrator, and her husband has been interested in wood engraving, typesetting, filmstrips, and book design. They illustrated Giants In The Sky (A Junior Literary Guild
selection), Richards, N. , Childrens Press, 1967.

BORNSCHLEGEL, Ruth
She spent her childhood in Denver, Colorado, graduated
from Harding College in Searcy, Arkansas, and did ad-
vanced study at the Kansas City Art Institute. Her home
has been in New York City where she has been a book
designer for a publishing firm. Prior to her career as
an illustrator, Miss Bornschlegel was a commercial
artist and worked in libraries. For children she illustrated The Bull In the Forest (A Junior Literary Guild
selection), Cohen, P. , Atheneum, 1969.

BOZZO, Frank
He was born in Chicago, attended New York's School

of Visual Arts, and has made his home in New York City.
His illustrations have appeared in both books and mag-
azines. For boys and girls he illustrated The Beasts Of
Never, McHargue, G. , Bobbs, 1968.

BRANSOM, Paul 1885-
He was born in Washington, D. C. Paul Bransom has been
called the "dean of American animal artists." When he
was seventeen, he was drawing for the New York Evening
Journal. At one time he had a studio in the New York
Zoological Park. Mr. Bransom has belonged to: Audubon
Artists, Society of Illustrators, Salmagundi Club, and the
American Water Color Society. He has lived on a ranch
in Jackson Hole, Wyoming and spent his summers at Can-
ada Lake in the Adirondacks. He illustrated: Biggest
Bear On Earth, McCracken, H. , Stokes, 1943; Marlin
Perkins' Zooparade, Perkins, R. , Rand, 1954.

ICB-1, ICB-2

BRIGGS, Raymond Redvers 1934-
Born in London, England, he grew up in Wimbledon where
he later attended the School of Art. He also studied at
the Slade School of Fine Art in London. Mr. Briggs has
continued to make his home near London. He has worked
in advertising in addition to illustrating books. He com-
piled and illustrated Fee Fi Fo Fum (Coward, 1964) which
was the runner-up for the Kate Greenaway Medal awarded
by England's Library Association for "the most distinguished work in the illustration of children's books." He
received the award for his illustrations in The Mother
Goose Treasury, Coward, 1966.   ICB-3

BROWN, Marcia Joan 1918-

She was born in Rochester, New York. She attended
the State College for Teachers in Albany, the Woodstock
School of Painting, and the New School for Social Research. She later worked with children in the New York
Public Library. After telling the story of Stone Soup
(Scribner, 1947), she decided to create a picture book
about it. She won the Caldecott Medal in 1955 for Cin-
derella, Scribner, 1954 and again in 1962 for Once a
Mouse, Scribner, 1961. Other titles include: Dick Whit-
tington And His Cat, Scribner, 1950; Felice, Scribner,
1958; How, Hippo!, Scribner, 1969; Little Carousel,
Scribner, 1946; The Neighbors, Scribner, 1967; Skipper
John's Cook, Junior Literary Guild and Scribner, 1951;
Tamarindo, Scribner, 1960. (Authors Of Books For
Young People-1964)   ICB-2, ICB-3

BRYSON, Bernarda 1903-

Born in Athens, Ohio, she studied at Ohio University,
Ohio State University, Cleveland School of Art, and the
New School for Social Research in New York. In addition to books, her illustrations have appeared in many
magazines. She has also worked on newspapers and
taught art. Her husband, Ben Shahn, has also been an
artist. They have lived in Roosevelt, New Jersey. For
young people she illustrated: Calendar Moon, Belting, N.,
Holt, 1964; The Return Of The Twelves, Clarke, P.,
Coward-McCann, 1962.   ICB-3

BURCKMYER, Elizabeth

She was born in California. She studied at Cornell

Burkert, Nancy Ekholm   1933-
University and later became an associate professor of
freehand drawing at the University.   She has also done
free-lance illustrating.   The book which she illustrated
for young people was The Makers Of Honey, Phillips,
M., Crowell, 1956.

BURKERT, Nancy Ekholm   1933-
Born in Sterling, Colorado, she grew up in the Midwest,
and graduated from the University of Wisconsin.   She
married artist Robert Burkert who has been an Associate
Professor of Art in Milwaukee.   Nancy Burkert has held
water color exhibitions in New York and Chicago.   She
illustrated The Nightingale (Andersen, H., Harper, 1965)
which was a 1965 Honor Book in the New York Herald
Tribune's Spring Book Festival.   It also received the
1966 Gold Medal awarded by the Society of Illustrators.
Other juvenile books which she illustrated include: A
Child's Calendar, Updike, J., Knopf, 1965; Jean-Claude's
Island, Carlson, N., Harper, 1963.   ICB-3

BURNINGHAM, John Mackintosh   1936-
Artist, illustrator, muralist, born in England.   He attended the Central School of Arts in Holborn, London, at
the age of twenty.   Mr. Burningham has resided in London where he has designed posters, murals, and illustrated books.   His work has also appeared in magazines.
He was awarded the 1963 Kate Greenaway Medal for his
first book Borka, Random, 1963.   He also wrote and
illustrated Harquin, Bobbs, 1967.   He illustrated Chitty
Chitty Bang Bang, Fleming, I., Random, 1964.   ICB-3

BURNS, Irene

   She was born in Boston, graduated from the Massachusetts
   College of Art, and has lived in Brookline. Irene Burns
   has taught art and painted portraits in addition to illustrating books. Her work can be found in Missing Melinda
   (A Junior Literary Guild selection), Jackson, J., Little,
   1967.

BURRIS, Burmah

   She graduated from college in Mississippi and continued
   her studies at the Art Institute in Chicago. Prior to
   working as a free-lance artist, she taught high school
   mathematics and science. Her work has appeared in
   adult books and magazines. Her first illustrations for
   young people appeared in Listen ! And Help Tell the
   Story, Carlson, B., Abingdon, 1965.

BURTON, Virginia Lee 1909-

   Born in Newton Centre, Massachusetts. She studied art
   and dancing at the California School of Fine Arts. She
   has taught dancing and contributed sketches to the Boston
   Transcript. She won the Caldecott Medal in 1943 for her
   book The Little House, Houghton, 1942. Juvenile titles
   include: Calico, The Wonder Horse, Houghton, 1950;
   Choo Choo, Houghton, 1937; Katy And The Big Snow,
   Houghton, 1943; Life Story, Houghton, 1962; Maybelle,
   The Cable Car, Houghton, 1952; Mike Mulligan And His
   Steam Shovel, Houghton, 1939. (Authors Of Books For
   Young People-1964)   ICB-1, ICB-2, ICB-3

CAMPBELL, Virginia 1914-

She was born in New Orleans, Louisiana and studied at
Gulf Park College, Gulfport, Mississippi, King-Smith
Studio School, Lisa Gardiner Ballet School, and the American Academy of Dramatic Arts.   Prior to painting, Virginia Campbell was in the theater where she appeared in
plays with both Judith Anderson and Eva LaGallienne.
She married John Becker and has lived in Rome.   She
illustrated her husband's book Near-Tragedy At The Water-
fall, Becker, J., Pantheon Bks., 1964.   ICB-2

CARLONI, Giancarlo

Illustrator and cartoonist.   Born in Italy, he has resided
in Milan.   Italian children have enjoyed his book illustrations.   Mr. Carloni later became a cartoonist and
with Giulio Cingoli was awarded the 1964 Prize Venezia.
Mr. Carloni collaborated with Mr. Cingoli to illustrate
his first book for children in America.   It was Gaetano
the Pheasant, Rocco, G., Harper, 1966.   ICB-3

CARY

His book for boys and girls was signed by his surname.
He studied at the Massachusetts School of Art.   In addi-
tion to illustrating books, he has also worked in adver-
tising.   The artist and his family have lived in West
Barnstable, Massachusetts where he has served as di-
rector of the Cape Cod Art Association and worked in the
Little Theatre group.   He illustrated Wonderful Stuff,
Russell, S., Rand, 1963.

CATHER, Carolyn

The daughter of an army officer, she spent her childhood in Japan and the Philippines. She studied at Duke
University in Durham, North Carolina. Following World
War II, she lived in Japan where she worked on the newspaper Stars And Stripes. Carolyn Cather later made her
home in New York City. Her work includes Women Of
Courage, Nathan, D., Random, 1964.

CELLINI, Eva   Joseph 1924-

Hungarian artists. They were born in Budapest where
they later attended the Academy of Fine Arts. Both became American citizens after coming to the United States
in 1956. The Cellinis have lived in Leonia, New Jersey.
Eva Cellini has enjoyed gardening and reading as hobbies.
For boys and girls she illustrated: All About Biology,
Glemser, B., Random, 1964; Partners In Nature, Dud-
ley, R., Funk & Wagnalls, 1965. His work includes:
Davy Jones' Haunted Locker, Arthur, R., ed., Random,
1965; Disaster At Johnstown, Dolson, H., Random, 1965.
                                                    ICB-3

CHAPPELL, Warren 1904-

Artist and designer, born in Richmond, Virginia. His
home has been in Norwalk, Connecticut. After graduating from the University of Richmond, he studied at the
Art Students League in New York and the Colorado
Springs Fine Arts Center. He did further study in Germany. Warren Chappell has been a typographer and
teacher in addition to illustrator. He wrote and illustrated The Nutcracker, Knopf, 1958. He also illus-

Chwast, Jacqueline   1932-
trated Prisoner Of The Indies (A Junior Literary Guild
selection), Household, G. , Little, 1968.

ICB-1, ICB-2, ICB-3

CHWAST, Jacqueline   1932-
She was born in Newark, New Jersey where she later
attended the Newark School of Fine and Industrial Art.
She also studied at the Art Students League in New York.
Her husband Seymour Chwast has been an artist and
graphic designer.   They have lived in New York City.
Her work includes: I Like You, Warburg, S. , Houghton,
1965; Wide Awake, and Other Poems, Livingston, M. ,
Harcourt, 1959.   ICB-3

CINGOLI, Giulio
Italian artist and cartoonist.   He has lived in Milan.   Mr.
Cingoli's work has appeared in books published for boys
and girls in Italy.   He has been interested in cartooning
and with Italian cartoonist Giancarlo Carloni, was the
recipient of the Prize Venzia in 1964.   Giulio Cingoli
and Mr. Carloni's book illustrations first appeared in
the United States in Gaetano the Pheasant, Rocco, G. ,
Harper, 1966.   ICB-3

COBER, Alan E.   1935-
He was born in New York City and studied at the University of Vermont, School of Visual Arts, New School
for Social Research, and Pratt Graphic Center in New
York.   In addition to books he has contributed illustrations to many magazines.   In 1965 the Artists Guild of
New York named Alan Cober Artist of the Year.   The

Connolly, Jerome Patrick 1931-

Cobers have lived in Ossining, New York. His work includes: Nothingatall, Nothingatall, Nothingatall, Smith, R. , Harper, 1965; The White Twilight, Polland, M. , Holt, 1965. ICB-3

CONNOLLY, Jerome Patrick 1931-
Born in Minneapolis, he studied at the University of Minnesota. He has painted diorama backgrounds for museums in addition to illustrating books for boys and girls. He met his wife, an editor, on one of his early assignments at the Illinois State Museum. He has been staff artist for the Natural Science for Youth Foundation and a member of the Society of Animal Artists. For young people he illustrated The Travels Of Monarch X, Hutchins, R. , Rand, 1966. ICB-3

COOLEY, Lydia
She attended the University of California at Los Angeles and the Art Students League in New York. Her paintings have been exhibited at the Santa Barbara Museum of Art and the Whitney Museum of American Art. Lydia Cooley has taught at the Ojai Valley School and has made her home in Santa Barbara. She illustrated Onion Journey, Cunningham, J. , Pantheon, 1967.

COONEY, Barbara 1917-
She was born in Brooklyn, New York and has lived in Illinois, Iowa, Massachusetts, and New York. Barbara Cooney graduated from Smith College in Northampton, Massachusetts. In 1959 she won the Caldecott Medal for her book Chanticleer And The Fox (Chaucer, G. , Crow-

ell, 1958). Her illustrations also appeared in The
Little Juggler (A Junior Literary Guild selection, Hastings House, 1961) which she adapted from an old French
legend. Other juvenile books which she illustrated include: Christmas, Crowell, 1967; Peacock Pie, De La
Mare, W., Knopf, 1961. (Authors Of Books For Young
People-1964)   ICB-1, ICB-2, ICB-3

COREY, Robert
Designer and illustrator, he has lived in Los Angeles.
He has received many awards both here and abroad for
his graphic designs. Robert Corey went to South America and visited the ancient Inca ruins of Peru which provided background material for some of his illustrations
in Tomasito and the Golden Llamas, Castellanos, J.,
Golden Gate Junior Books, 1968.

CRICHLOW, Ernest T. 1914-
Born in Brooklyn, New York, he studied at the Commercial Illustration School of Art and the Art Students
League in New York. His first one-man show was held
in 1953. He has taught painting at Brighton Art Center
and has made his home in Brooklyn. His work includes:
Corrie And The Yankee, Levy, M., Viking, 1959; Lincoln's Birthday, Bulla, C., Crowell, 1965.   ICB-3

CROSBY, John
He was born in Toronto, Canada where he later studied
at the University. He began his career in art by drawing pictures of birds for a nature magazine. Later his
work appeared in books, and he created natural history

film strips for the National Film Board.   Prior to becoming a museologist with the National Parks Branch
of the Department of Indian Affairs and Northern Devel-
opment, he worked in Ottawa as Artist-Naturalist of the
Zoology Department of the National Museum.   He illustrated Book of American Birds, May, C. , St. Martin's,
1967.

CUFFARI, Richard
Born in Brooklyn, New York, he later graduated from
Pratt Institute.   His paintings have been exhibited in
many galleries of New York and were also included in
the United States Information Agency's Graphic Arts-USA
Exhibit which were shown in Russia.   He married an artist and has lived in Brooklyn.   The book which he illustrated for boys and girls was Nothing Is Impossible (A
Junior Literary Guild selection), Aldis, D. , Atheneum,
1969.

DARWIN, Beatrice
Born in Boston, she attended the Massachusetts School
of Art where she later did graduate work on a scholarship.   She also studied abroad in Sweden.   She married
calligrapher (handwriting artist) and graphic artist Leonard Darwin and has lived in California.   She illustrated
Pete's Puddle, Foster, J. , Houghton, 1950.

DARWIN, Leonard
His early years were spent in Beverly and Needham,
Massachusetts.   He attended the Massachusetts School
of Art in Boston where he studied advertising and design.

He married an illustrator and has lived in Danville, California. In addition to illustrating children's books, Len Darwin has worked as an art director, fashion and design instructor, and map draftsman. He has also worked in advertising. For young people he illustrated: What Makes A Plane Fly? (A Junior Literary Guild selection), Corbett, S. , Atlantic, 1967; What Makes TV Work?, Corbett, S. , Little, 1965.

D'ATTILIO, Anthony

A citizen of the United States, Anthony D'Attilio was born in Italy. He has worked in New York City at the American Museum of Natural History as an Associate in the Department of Living Invertebrates. In addition to a career as an artist, he has also been a writer. His speciality has been in writing about and drawing marine mollusks (shellfish). The artist's work has appeared in books and scientific papers. For young people he illustrated Octopus Lives In The Ocean, Stephens, W. , Holiday, 1968.

D'AULAIRE, Ingri (Mortenson) 1904- Edgar Parin 1898-

Husband-wife team. Ingri Mortenson was born in Norway, and Edgar, who was the son of an Italian portrait painter, was born in Switzerland. They met when both were studying art in Paris. After their marriage, they arrived in the United States. They have achieved distinction in their early picture books by drawing directly on lithograph stone. They have lived on a farm in Wilton, Connecticut. The Caldecott Medal was awarded to their

book <u>Abraham Lincoln</u>, Doubleday, 1939. They wrote:
<u>Animals Everywhere</u>, Doubleday, 1940; <u>Ingri and Edgar</u>
<u>Parin D'Aulaire's Book Of Greek Myths</u>, Doubleday,
1962; <u>Buffalo Bill</u>, Junior Literary Guild and Doubleday,
1952; <u>Ola</u>, Doubleday, 1932. (<u>Authors Of Books For</u>
<u>Young People</u>-1964)   ICB-1, ICB-2, ICB-3

DAVIS, Bette

Born in Joplin, Missouri, she studied at Pratt Institute.
She was head of the art department (Special Services)
in the U. S. Marine Corps Woman's Reserve during World
War II. Her work has appeared in both science books
and encyclopedias. She has enjoyed painting the ocean
near her home in New Jersey. Her illustrations appeared in <u>Twice Queen Of France: Anne Of Brittany</u>
(A Junior Literary Guild selection), Butler, M., Funk,
1967.

DE LARREA, Victoria

She was born in New York City, at nineteen traveled
around the world on a cargo ship as an officer-stew-
ardess, and later attended Queen's College in New York.
She married a photographer and has lived on Long Island. Her illustrations have appeared in many books.
These include: <u>Miss Know It All</u>, York, C., Watts,
1966; <u>The Pheasant On Route Seven</u>, Starbird, K.,
Lippincott, 1968; <u>Philip And The Pooka</u>, Green, K.,
Lippincott, 1966.

DE PAOLA, Tomie

Illustrator, instructor, born in Meriden, Connecticut.

He graduated from Pratt Institute in Brooklyn, New
York.   He has taught art at Newton College of the Sacred
Heart in Massachusetts and at San Francisco College for
Women.   He has lived in New York, Connecticut, and
California.   He wrote and illustrated Wonderful Dragon
of Timlin, Bobbs, 1966.   He also illustrated Tricky
Peik and Other Picture Tales, Hardendorff, J. , ed. ,
Lippincott, 1967.   ICB-3

DEVLIN, Harry

He and his wife Wende have created picture books for
boys and girls.   Mr. Devlin has been a freelance illustrator.   The Devlins have lived in Mountainside, New
Jersey.   Their work includes: Aunt Agatha, There's a
Lion Under the Couch!, Van Nostrand, 1968; The
Knobby Boys to the Rescue, Parents' Magazine Press,
1965.

DILLON, Corinne Boyd

She was born in Louisville, Kentucky and grew up in
Kentucky, Minnesota, and New York.   She attended
Friends School in Providence, Rhode Island and the
Barnard School for Girls in New York.   Corinne Dillon
also studied at Académie Julian in Paris.   Her home
has been in New York City.   She illustrated A Letter
For Cathy, Hitte, K. , Abingdon, 1953.   ICB-2

DOLEZAL, Carroll

Born in New London, Connecticut, she studied at the
Rhode Island School of Design and at the Kansas City
Art Institute.   As a member of the European Honors

Program, she spent a year of study in Italy. Mrs.
Dolezal has been a designer for Hallmark Cards in Kansas City, Missouri and a high school art teacher in
Texas. She and her husband Dr. Charles H. Dolezal,
a psychologist, have lived in Austin. She illustrated
A Sky Full Of Dragons (A Junior Literary Guild selection), Wright, M. , Steck, 1969.

DOREMUS, Robert
His paintings of New York scenes were sold in order to
earn money to attend Pratt Institute in Brooklyn. Bob
Doremus served overseas as a photographic technician
with the Air Force during World War II. The Doremus
family has lived in Union Springs, New York where the
author has enjoyed sailing as a hobby. His work for
children includes: John Fitch: Steamboat Boy, Stevenson, A. , Bobbs, 1966; Osceola: Young Seminole Indian,
Clark, E. , Bobbs, 1965.

DOWD, Victor
He grew up in France and later came to America where
he made his home in Westport, Connecticut. He studied
at Pratt Institute in Brooklyn, New York and has been
both a book illustrator and advertising artist. Mr. Dowd
has enjoyed model-railroading as a hobby. For boys
and girls he illustrated Getting To Know France, Wallace, J. , Coward, 1962.

DUNNINGTON, Tom
He grew up in Duluth, Minnesota and Iowa City, Iowa.

Duvoisin, Roger Antoine 1904-

Following service in the Marine Corps, he studied art
at the University of Iowa, John Herron School of Art in
Indianapolis, and at Chicago's American Academy of
Art. He and his wife have lived in Elmhurst, Illinois.
He illustrated The Story Of Old Ironsides (A Junior Literary Guild selection), Richards, N. , Childrens Press,
1967.

DUVOISIN, Roger Antoine 1904-

Author-illustrator. He was born in Switzerland. He re-
ceived his education in Switzerland and France. Mr.
Duvoisin worked in design in Geneva, Lyons, and Paris.
After arriving in America, he has been a painter, de-
signer, and illustrator. His titles include: A For The
Ark, Lothrop, 1952; And There Was America, Knopf,
1938; Christmas Whale, Knopf, 1945; The Happy Hunter,
Lothrop, 1961; House Of Four Seasons, Lothrop, 1956;
Lonely Veronica, Knopf, 1963; Petunia, I Love You,
Knopf, 1965; Spring Snow, Knopf, 1963. Also he illus-
trated Alvin Tresselt's White Snow, Bright Snow (Loth-
rop, 1947) which won the Caldecott Medal in 1948.
(Authors Of Books For Young People-1964)

ICB-1, ICB-2, ICB-3

EATON, John 1942-

Canadian artist, born in Ottawa. He received his ed-
ucation in Canada and at the High Mowing School in Wil-
ton, New Hampshire. He has traveled throughout several
European countries and studied marble sculpturing in
Italy. At one time he lived in Fiesole near Florence,
Italy. For children he illustrated Fairy Tales, Cum-

mings, E. , Harcourt, 1965.

EDWARDS, Peter 1934-
   He was born in London and later studied art there at
   the Regent Street Polytechnic. Following military service, he began his illustrating career in Sweden. Peter
   Edwards and his wife who has also been an artist have
   lived at Stansted Mountfitchet in Essex. He illustrated
   Seals For Sale, Memling, C. , Abelard-Schuman, 1963.

EGGENHOFER, Nicholas
   Born in Bavaria, he came to the United States when he
   was sixteen. He later made his home in West Milford,
   New Jersey. Prior to coming to America, he enjoyed
   reading about the old West which has been the subject
   for many of his illustrations. For young people he illustrated Geronimo: Wolf Of The Warpath, Moody, R. ,
   Random, 1958.

EICKE, Edna
   Born in Montclair, New Jersey, she received her education in New York City at the Parsons School of Design.
   She married artist Tom Funk and has resided in Westport, Connecticut. She has designed covers for the New
   Yorker magazine and has enjoyed collecting primitive
   art and antique toys as hobbies. She wrote and illustrated The Children Who Got Married, Simon, 1969.

EITZEN, Allan
   He was born in Minnesota and later studied art in Minneapolis. He has worked in a Pennsylvania religious

publishing firm where he learned about printing and de-
sign.   The Eitzens have lived on a farm in Pennsylvania.
He has often used his own children as models for his
book illustrations.   His work includes: Kish's Colt, Agle,
N. , Seabury Press, 1968; What's That Noise?, Kauffman,
L. , Lothrop, 1966.

EMBERLEY, Ed 1931-

He graduated from the Massachusetts School of Art and
attended the Rhode Island School of Design after World
War II.   His home has been in Millis, Massachusetts.
In 1968 he was awarded the Caldecott Medal for Drummer
Hoff (A Junior Literary Guild selection), Emberley, B. ,
adapted by, Prentice-Hall, 1967.   He also illustrated:
The Big Dipper, Branley, F. , Crowell, 1962; Green Says
Go, Little, 1968; The Parade Book (A Junior Literary
Guild selection), Little, 1962; The Wing On A Flea,
Little, 1961.   (Authors Of Books For Young People-1964)

ICB-3

ERDOES, Richard 1912-

He was born in Vienna and studied at the Art Academies
of Berlin, Paris, and Vienna.   He later became a United
States citizen.   His work includes: murals for the Rich-
mond, Virginia Museum of Fine Arts and the Grace Line
ship "Santa Maria" and illustrations for Life magazine.
His interests have been photography, camping, and skiing.
For boys and girls he illustrated The Cat and the Devil,
Joyce, J. , Dodd, 1934.   He also wrote and illustrated
A Picture History of Ancient Rome, Macmillan, 1967.

ICB-3

ETS, Marie Hall 1895-

Born in Wisconsin, she studied at the University of Chicago, the Art Institute, and Columbia University. At one
time she did social work and lived for a year in Czechoslovakia. She married Harold Ets who was on the staff
of Loyola University School of Medicine. In 1960 she
was awarded the Caldecott Medal for her illustrations in
Nine Days To Christmas (Viking, 1959) which she wrote
with Aurora Labastida. Juvenile titles include: Beasts
And Nonsense, Junior Literary Guild and Viking, 1952;
Gilberto And The Wind, Viking, 1963; Just Me, Viking,
1965; Mister Penny, Viking, 1935; Talking Without Words,
Viking, 1968. (Authors Of Books For Young People-1964)

ICB-1, ICB-2, ICB-3

FAULKNER, John

Cartoonist-illustrator. Prior to a career as an artist,
John Faulkner studied to be a college professor. The
Faulkner family has lived near Chicago in Glen Ellyn,
Illinois. They have enjoyed golf, skiing, and tennis as
special interests. For boys and girls he illustrated: The
Little Band & the Inaugural Parade (A Junior Literary
Guild selection), Moore, M. , Whitman, 1968; Who Was
Tricked?, Bowman, J. , Whitman, 1966.

FEASER, Daniel David 1920-

He was born in Dauphin, Pennsylvania and later attended
Westminster Choir College in Princeton, New Jersey and
the Philadelphia Museum School of Art. He has been an
exhibit artist and designer for the Museums Branch of
the National Park Service. His home has been in Fairfax

County, Virginia. His work includes: A History Of Fire-
arms, Peterson, H. , Scribner, 1961; A History Of Knives,
Peterson, H. , Scribner, 1966.   ICB-3

FEELINGS, Tom
He grew up in Brooklyn, New York and later studied at
the School of Visual Arts. In 1964 he served as an art-
ist with the Ghanian Government Publishing House in Accra,
West Africa. For young people he illustrated To Be A
Slave, Lester, J. , Dial, 1968.

FEGIZ, Rita Fava 1932-
Italian artist and portrait painter, born in Rome. Her
childhood was spent in Italy, and she came to the United
States when she was thirteen. She attended high school
in Philadelphia, Pennsylvania and later studied at the
Philadelphia Museum School of Art. She returned to Rome
and married architect Carlo Fegiz in 1962. She has done
portraits of children in addition to book illustrations. Juvenile books which she has illustrated include: Gift From
the Bride, Cretan, G. , Little, 1964; Piccolina and the
Easter Bells, Priolo, P. , Little, 1962.   ICB-3

FERGUSON, Walter W. 1930-
He was born in New York City and has lived in Brooklyn.
Prior to attending Pratt Institute, he studied art at Yale
University. He has traveled throughout the United States
and Canada observing and sketching birds and animals.
His paintings have been exhibited in many museums.
Walter Ferguson has illustrated books for both children and

adults, and his work has appeared in Audubon Magazine,
Life, and Sports Illustrated.   He has been an artist with
New York's American Museum of Natural History and a
member of the Society of Animal Artists.   For children
he illustrated: Barn Swallow, Sears, P. , Holiday, 1955;
When Animals Change Clothes, May, C. , Holiday, 1965.

ICB-2

FETZ, Ingrid 1915-
She was born in New York City where she later studied
at Columbia University and at the Workshop School of
Advertising and Editorial Art.   Her father, born in
Switzerland, was an engineer and photographer; and her
mother, graduate of Pratt Institute, was a children's li-
brarian.   In addition to teaching art to boys and girls,
Ingrid Fetz has been Director of the Cambridge, Mass-
achusetts Art Center for Children.   She has lived in
Ossining, New York.   Her work includes: The Adven-
ture of Walter, Clymer, E. , Atheneum, 1965; Laughable
Limericks, Brewton, S & I. , comp. , Crowell, 1965.

ICB-3

FIAMMENGHI, Gioia 1929-
She was born in New York City where she later studied
at the Art Students League and Parsons School of Design.
While she was a student at Parsons, she traveled in
France and Italy.   She also spent several summers painting and drawing in Colombia, South America.   She married Guido Caputo and has lived in Monte Carlo, Monaco.
Several of her paintings have been exhibited in the American Consulate in Nice.   Her work includes: A Book To

Fischer, Ann A.

Begin On Libraries, Bartlett, S. , Holt, 1964; Noisy Nancy
Norris, Gaeddert, L. , Doubleday, 1965; Papa Albert,
Moore, L. , Atheneum, 1964.   ICB-2, ICB-3,

FISCHER, Ann A.

She was born in Peoria, Illinois.   At one time she lived
in Italy where she was an art instructor and designed
covers for magazines.   Miss Fischer has also worked in
advertising and public relations.   Private collectors own
many of her paintings.   For children she illustrated The
Bat Book, Kohn, B. , Hawthorn Books, 1967.

FISK, Nicholas

This illustrator has also been an author of fact and fiction for boys and girls (including Richthofen, The Red
Baron, Coward, 1968).   He served in the British Royal
Air Force during World War II.   For young people he
illustrated Tea With Mr. Timothy, Morgan, G. , Little,
1966.

FLEISHMAN, Seymour 1918-

He has always lived in or near Chicago where he was
born.   He received his education at the Art Institute in
Chicago.   In addition to illustrating books, he has worked
in advertising.   Seymour Fleishman served in Australia
and New Guinea during World War II.   He illustrated:
Bunny In The Honeysuckle Patch, Woolley, C. , Morrow,
1965; Know Your Bible, Jones, M. , Rand, 1965.

                                           ICB-2, ICB-3

FLOYD, Gareth

He was born in Lancashire, England and studied art at
Lowestoft, Guilford and Brighton Colleges of Art. Mr.
Floyd has done both book and magazine illustrations and
in addition has taught at Leiscester College of Art in
England. His work includes: Flight to the Forest, Wil-
lard, B., Doubleday, 1967; Second-Hand Family, Parker,
R., Bobbs, 1967.

FRAME, Paul 1913-

He was born in Riderwood, Maryland and later studied
at Columbia University and the National Academy of Design in New York City. He has been an artist for a
large department store and has worked at Friends Semin-
ary. His work includes: Casey At The Bat, Thayer, E.,
Prentice-Hall, 1964; Katie John, Calhoun, M., Harper,
1960.   ICB-3

FRASCINO, Edward

Born in New York, as a student he spent several months
in Mexico. He has also traveled throughout the Orient.
His cartoons and drawings have appeared in the New York
Times, Saturday Review, and the New Yorker magazine.
Mr. Frascino has also been a painter and has done fig-
urative work in oils or acrylic. The first children's
book which he illustrated was Say Something, Stolz, M.,
Harper, 1968. He also illustrated Dragons Of The Queen,
Stolz, M., Harper, 1969.

FREUND, Rudolf 1915-

He was born in Philadelphia where he later studied at the

Galster, Robert 1928-

museum School of Industrial Art and the Graphic Sketch
Club. He also attended Pennsylvania's Academy of the
Fine Arts and the Art Students League in New York. His
home has been in East Haddam, Connecticut. He has illustrated books for both adults and children and has become well-known for his painting and illustration in the
field of natural history. Mr. Freund's work has also
appeared in Life magazine ("The World We Live In").
For boys and girls he illustrated Rainbow Book Of Nature,
Peattie, D., World, 1957.   ICB-1, ICB-2

GALSTER, Robert 1928-

He was born in Dollville, Illinois, spent his childhood in
Mansifeld, Ohio, and later made his home in New York
City. Mr. Glaster studied at the Parsons School of Design. When he was in the Army Engineers in Europe,
he became interested in poster design and later worked
in poster design for the theater on Broadway. He has
also painted murals in various hotels. He illustrated
Find Out By Touching, Showers, P., Crowell, 1961.
                                         ICB-3

GEARY, Clifford N. 1916-

Born in Somerville, Massachusetts, he studied at Rindge
Technical High School in Cambridge, the Massachusetts
School of Art in Boston, Pratt Institute in Brooklyn, and
the Art Students League in New York. He has been in-
terested in camping, photography, and American history.
Mr. Geary has lived in Brooklyn and Astoria, New York.
He illustrated Wonder World of Microbes (new second
edition), Grant, M., McGraw, 1964.   ICB-2

GEER, Charles 1922-

Born on Long Island, New York, he studied at Dartmouth
College in Hanover, New Hampshire and at Pratt Institute
in Brooklyn, New York. During World War II, he served on a Navy destroyer. In 1952 he traveled throughout Europe. Mr. Geer and his family have lived near
Lebanon, New Jersey. His work includes: Sam And
The Colonels, Bradbury, B. , Macrae Smith, 1966; Miss
Pickerell Goes On A Dig, MacGregor, E. , McGraw,
1966.   ICB-2, ICB-3

GEKIERE, Madeleine 1919-

She was born in Zurich, Switzerland and later studied at
the Sorbonne in Paris and at the Art Students League in
New York. She came to the United States in 1940 and
decided to become an artist. Her home has been in New
York City where she has taught art at New York University. Books which she illustrated include John J. Plenty
and Fiddler Dan, Ciardi, J. , Lippincott, 1963. She
wrote and illustrated Who Gave Us... Peacocks? Planes?
& Ferris Wheels?, Pantheon, 1953.   ICB-2, ICB-3

GENIA see WENNERSTROM, Genia Katherine

GILL, Margery Jean 1925-

Born in Scotland, she grew up in Middlesex, England.
She attended the Harrow School of Art and the Royal
College of Art where she studied engraving and etching.
She has taught art in addition to her work in book illus-
tration. One of her books for young people was Requiem
For A Princess (A Junior Literary Guild selection),

Arthur, R., Atheneum, 1967.

GIOVANOPOULOS, Paul

He has lived in New York City where he has been a painter.   The first children's book that he illustrated was
written about a boy who lived in Brooklyn.   It was How
Many Miles to Babylon?, Fox, P., David White, 1967.

GLANZMAN, Louis S.   1922-

He was born in Baltimore, Maryland, grew up in Virginia,
and has lived in Sayville, Long Island, New York.   He
has created comic strips and magazine covers.   His portraits have appeared on the cover of Time magazine and
in the Ford Theater Museum in Washington D. C.   Mr.
Glanzman was chosen by the Society of Illustrators to
tour the Far East for the USAF in 1954, and his paintings have been exhibited in the Pentagon.   For children
he illustrated: The Chagres, Latham, J., Garrard, 1964;
Pippi Longstocking, Lindgren, A., Viking, 1950.   ICB-3

GLASER, Milton   1929-

He was born in New York City, grew up in the Bronx,
and graduated from Cooper Union.   He studied in Italy
at the Bologna Academy of Fine Arts on a Fulbright grant.
With Seymour Chwast he founded the Push Pin Studios.
Mr. Glaser has been an instructor at New York City's
School of Visual Arts.   He has designed book jackets,
illustrated books, and worked in advertising.   He has been
the recipient of the Gold Medal of the Art Directors Club
and the Society of Illustrators.   For children he illustrated: Cats And Bats And Things With Wings, Aiken, C.,

Atheneum, 1965; Smallest Elephant In The World, Tresselt,
A. , Knopf, 1959. With his wife Shirley Glaser he wrote
and illustrated If Apples Had Teeth, Knopf, 1960. ICB-3

GOBBATO, Imero 1923-
Born in Milan, Italy, he studied at Liceo Artistico and
the Academy of Fine Arts in Milan and graduated from
Venice's Royal Institute of Art. He has been a naval
architect and set designer for the motion picture industry
in addition to his work as an illustrator of books for
young people. He and his wife have lived in Camden,
Maine. His book for young people was The King With
Six Friends, Williams, J. , Parents, 1968.   ICB-3

GOLDSTEIN, Nathan
He grew up in Chicago and studied at the Chicago Art In-
stitute. Later he lived in the East and taught painting
and drawing at the New England School of Art and Boston
University. He married a painter, and they have lived
in Waban, Massachusetts. His work includes: Abraham
Lincoln: Man Of Courage, Bailey, B. , Houghton, 1960;
Adlai Stevenson: Young Ambassador, Ward, M. , Bobbs,
1967; Heartsease (A Junior Literary Guild selection),
Dickinson, P. , Atlantic-Little, 1969.

GONZALEZ, Xavier
He was born in Almeria, Spain and came to the United
States in 1921. His sculpture and paintings are in the
collections of the Whitney and Metropolitan Museums in
New York, and Delgado Museum in New Orleans, and the
Museum of Fine Arts in Seattle. Mr. González has taught

in universities and has received awards from the National
Academy of Arts and the American Academy of Arts and
Letters.   He married painter Ethel Edwards and has
lived in New York City.   His work includes He Who Saw
Everything: The Epic Of Gilgamesh, Feagles, A. , ed. ,
Scott, 1966.

GOODENOW, Girard 1912-
He was born in Chicago and later studied at the Art
Institute of Chicago and the Art Students League in New
York.   His illustrations have appeared in Woman's Day
and the Saturday Evening Post.   He also has done ad-
vertising art.   His work for young people includes: The
Bug Club Book, Conklin, G. , Holiday, 1966; Smoke Above
The Lane, DeJong, M. , Harper, 1951.   ICB-2

GOREY, Edward St. John 1925-
Artist and writer, born in Chicago, Illinois.   He received
his B. A. degree from Harvard.   In addition to illustrating books by different authors, Edward Gorey has also
written and illustrated his own books for children which
include The Bug Book, Random, 1960.   He also illustrated: The King Who Saved Himself From Being Saved,
Ciardi, J. , Lippincott, 1965; Three Ladies Beside The
Sea, Levine, R. , Atheneum, 1963.   ICB-3

GORMAN, Terry see POWERS, Richard M.

GORSLINE, Douglas Warner 1913-
Illustrator, writer, he was born in Rochester, New York
and has lived in New York City.   He attended the Yale

Grabianski, Janusz 1929-

School of Fine Arts and the Art Students, League in New
York. Mr. Gorsline has done both book and magazine
illustration, worked in advertising art, and written books.
He has been the recipient of many art awards and has
won national recognition for his "Portrait of Thomas
Wolfe." His work has appeared in many galleries and
museums. For young people he illustrated: Story of
Good Queen Bess, Malkus, A. , Grosset, 1953; Trust
Thyself, Wood, J. Pantheon, 1964.   ICB-2, ICB-3

GRABIANSKI, Janusz 1929-

He was born in Szamotuly, Poland and studied at the
Academy of Art in Cracow and Warsaw. His likes have
been listed as: children, flowers, animals, birds, and
fast cars. He has designed two series of stamps which
have been issued in Poland. The Gold Medal of the 1960
Milan Triennale was awarded to Mr. Grabianski. For
young people he illustrated: The Big Book Of Animal
Stories, Green, M. , comp. and ed. , Watts, 1961; The
Big Book Of Wild Animals, Green, M. , Watts, 1964. He
also wrote and illustrated: Birds, Watts, 1968; Dogs,
Watts, 1968.   ICB-3

GRABOFF, Abner 1919-

He was born in New York City and grew up in East
Orange, New Jersey. He studied at Brooklyn Museum
Art School. In addition to illustrating books for boys and
girls he has been a commercial artist. He has lived
near New York City. The first book he illustrated for
young people was The Sun Looks Down (Schlein, M. ,

Abelard, 1954) which was selected as one of the ten best
illustrated books of 1954 by the New York Times. He
also illustrated: Heat, Liss, H., Coward-McCann, 1965;
Mrs. McGarrity's Peppermint Sweater (A Junior Literary
Guild selection), Holl, A., Lothrop, 1966.   ICB-3

GREENWALD, Sheila 1934-

She was born in New York City and graduated from Sarah
Lawrence College. She has written for adults, and her
work has appeared in Harper's magazine. She married
surgeon George Green, and they have lived in New York
City. Her work includes: The Boy Who Couldn't Make
Up His Mind, Colman, H., Macmillan, 1965; The Re-
markable Ramsey, Rinkoff, B., Morrow, 1965.   ICB-3

GRETZER, John

He spent his early years in Council Bluffs, Iowa. He
received his education at the University of Omaha and the
Kansas City Art Institute. The artist served as a combat
artist with the U. S. Coast Guard during World War II.
Mr. Gretzer has been an art director for a publishing
firm in Philadelphia. His favorite hobby has been wood-
carving. For young people he illustrated: Drummer Of
Vincennes, Sentman, G., Winston, 1952; Hans Christian
Andersen: Fairy Tale Author, Garst, S., Houghton,
1965; The Other Side Of The Fence, Cone, M., Houghton,
1967.

GRIFALCONI, Ann 1929-

Native New Yorker, illustrator, and art instructor. A
graduate of Cooper Union, she also studied at Hunter

Grossman, Nancy S. 1940-

College, New York University, and the University of
Cincinnati in Ohio. In addition to teaching art, she has
illustrated books and magazines. Miss Grifalconi was
the 1966 Newbery Medal runner-up for her woodcuts in
The Jazz Man, Weik, M. , Atheneum, 1966. She also
wrote and illustrated City Rhythms, Bobbs, 1965.   ICB-3

GROSSMAN, Nancy S. 1940-
Born in New York City, she grew up on a farm in
Oneonta, New York, and later spent a year in Puerto
Rico. She attended the University of Arizona in Tucson
and graduated from Pratt Institute. She was the recipient
of both the Contemporary Achievement Award in Fine Arts
and a foreign travel scholarship from Pratt. Miss Grossman studied in Italy and Spain and was awarded a Guggenheim Fellowship in 1965. Her paintings have been exhibited in several one-man shows. For boys and girls
she illustrated: Did You Carry the Flag Today, Charley?,
Caudill, R. , Holt, 1966; Patricia Crosses Town, Baum,
B. , Knopf, 1965.   ICB-3

GWYNNE, Fred
He was born in New York City. Mr. Gwynne graduated
from Harvard. In addition to being an artist, he has also
been an actor and was in the television series "Car 54-
Where Are You!" He has lived in Bedford Hills, New
York. For boys and girls he illustrated The Battle of
the Frogs and the Mice, Martin, G. , Dodd, 1962.

HAAS, Irene 1929-
She was born and grew up in New York City. She atten-

ded college in North Carolina, Pratt Institute in Brooklyn,
and the Art Students League in New York City. She has
designed china and wallpaper and has also worked in advertising. Her home has been in Jamaica, New York.
For children she illustrated: Tatsinda, Enright, E. ,
Harcourt, 1963; Zeee, Enright, E. Harcourt, 1965.

ICB-2, ICB-3

HADER, Berta (Hoerner) Elmer 1889-
Husband-wife team, authors, illustrators. Born in Mex-
ico, Berta Hader studied journalism at the University of
Washington and attended the California School of Design.
She married artist Elmer Hader. Born in Pajaro, California, Mr. Hader studied in Paris, France. After service in World War I, he married Berta Hoerner. In
1949 the Haders won the Caldecott Medal for their book
The Big Snow, Macmillan, 1948. Other titles include:
Big City, Macmillan, 1947; Friendly Phoebe, Macmillan,
1953; Little Antelope, Macmillan, 1962; Midget And
Bridget, Macmillan, 1934; Wish On The Moon, Macmillan,
1954. (Authors Of Books For Young People-1964)

ICB-1, ICB-2, ICB-3

HALEY, Gail
She was born in Charlotte, North Carolina and studied
at the Richmond Professional Institute and the University
of Virginia. In addition to being an artist, Mrs. Haley
has been an art director and an apprentice in a print
shop. She has lived in New York City. For boys and
girls she illustrated Koalas, Kohn, B. , Prentice-Hall,
1965.

HAMBERGER, John F.   1934-

He was born in Jamaica, Long Island, New York, and
studied at New York City's School of Visual Arts. His
interest in nature and wildlife later led to his work in the
Museum of Natural History Nature and Science publication.
His work has also appeared in Boys' Life magazine.   Mr.
Hamberger has belonged to the Society of Animal Illus-
trators, the Zoological Society, and the Museum of Nat-
ural History.   For children he illustrated Raccoons, Kohn,
B., Prentice-Hall, 1968.   He also wrote and illustrated
The Day the Sun Disappeared, Norton, 1964.   ICB-3

HANDFORTH, Thomas Schofield 1897-1948

Born in Tacoma, Washington, he studied art in New York
and Paris.   He was awarded the Caldecott Medal in 1939
for his book, Mei Li (Doubleday, 1938), which was created when Mr. Handforth lived in Peking, China.   Before
his death in 1948, Mr. Handforth resided in California.
His work has been exhibited in many great museums including the Metropolitan Museum of Art in New York,
the Chicago Art Institute, and the Fogg Art Museum in
Cambridge, Massachusetts.   He wrote and illustrated
Mei Li, Doubleday, 1938.   (Authors Of Books For Young
People-1964)   ICB-1, ICB-2

HAYNES, Robert

He was born in Colorado and at one time lived in London,
England.   After graduating from Colorado College he did
graduate work at Columbia and London Universities.   He
married writer Nanda Weedon Ward, and together they
wrote: Beau, Ariel, 1957; Wellington and the Witch,

Henneberger, Robert G.   1921-
  Hastings House, 1959.   Bob Haynes also illustrated
  Mister Mergatroid, Ward, N. , Hastings House, 1960.

HENNEBERGER, Robert G.   1921-
  He grew up in Baltimore, Maryland where he was born.
  The artist served as a medical illustrator at Bethesda
  Hospital with the U.S. Navy during World War II and
  also was stationed in the South Pacific.   After the war,
  Mr. Henneberger graduated from the Rhode Island School
  of Design and later made his home in East Providence,
  Rhode Island.   His book illustrations include: Beatinest
  Boy, Stuart, J. , McGraw, 1953; A Ride With Huey The
  Engineer, Stuart, J. , McGraw, 1966.   ICB-2

HIDA, Keiko   1913-
  Japanese artist and photographer, born in Osaka.   Her
  career began as an instructor of classical Japanese
  dance, and she later founded her own art school in
  Tokyo.   She has become well-known for her exquisite
  calligraphy in addition to her essays and poetry.   She
  has also designed kimonos.   Keiko Hida has traveled
  and lectured throughout America and Europe.   For boys
  and girls she illustrated The Prancing Pony, DeForest,
  C. (adapted by), Walker, 1967.

HINES, Bob
  He has been an artist with the United States Fish and
  Wildlife Service and has designed several wildlife postage stamps for the U.S. government.   He has also illustrated adult books in addition to ones for boys and girls
  including Honker, McClung, R. , Morrow, 1965.

HNIZDOVSKY, Jacques

He was born in the Ukraine and later came to the United
States where he became an American citizen in 1954.
He received his art education in Warsaw and in Zagreb.
Well-known as a graphic artist, his work has been ex-
hibited in museums throughout this country and in inter-
national traveling exhibitions.   For children he illustra-
ted The Auk, The Dodo, And The Oryx, Silverberg, R.,
Crowell, 1967.

HODGES, David

Born in Brooklyn, New York, he studied at the Leonardo
da Vinci School of Fine Arts and the Art Students League
in New York.   Mr. Hodges has contributed cartoons to
both the Saturday Evening Post and New Yorker magazines.   He has also worked in advertising agencies.   His
home has been in Jamaica on Long Island.   For young
people he illustrated Nat Love, Negro Cowboy, Felton,
H., Dodd, 1969.

HOGROGIAN, Nonny 1932-

She has lived in New York City where she was born.
She graduated from Hunter College and also studied at
the New School for Social Research in New York City.
In 1966 she was awarded the Caldecott Medal for her
illustrations in Always Room For One More, Alger, L.,
Holt, 1965.   She also illustrated: Gaelic Ghosts (A
Junior Literary Guild selection), Alger, L., Holt, 1964;
Hand In Hand We'll Go, Burns, R., Crowell, 1965.
(Authors Of Books For Young People-1967)   ICB-3

HOLLING, Lucille (Webster) 1900-

Artist and designer, born in Valparaiso, Indiana. She studied at the Chicago Art Institute. She married author-illustrator Holling Clancy Holling and has lived in Pasadena, California. Mrs. Holling has designed costumes, illustrated for fashion publications, and has also been a ceramics instructor for the Red Cross. With her husband she illustrated: Book Of Cowboys, Holling, H. , Platt, 1936; Pagoo, Holling, H. , Houghton, 1957.

ICB-1, ICB-2, ICB-3

HOWARD, Rob

The artist and his wife Veronica have resided in New York's East Village. The recipient of many awards, Rob Howard has been commended for his illustrations in The Little Pig In The Cupboard, Buckley, H. , Lothrop, 1968.

HUTCHINS, Pat

Born in Yorkshire, England, she studied at Leeds College of Art. She illustrated her first book for children on a visit to New York. She began drawing at the age of seven when she was encouraged by a couple "who gave her a bar of chocolate for each picture." She wrote and illustrated Rosie's Walk, Macmillan, 1968.

HUTCHISON, Paula A. 1905-

Born in Helena, Montana, she grew up in the Pacific Northwest. She attended the University of Washington in Seattle and Pratt Institute in Brooklyn, New York. She also studied design in Florence, London, and Paris.

Hutchinson, William M.   1916-

She and her husband have lived near Matawan, New Jer-
sey.   For young people she illustrated: Abe Lincoln
Gets His Chance, Cavanah, F. , Rand, 1959; Animals On
The Move, Sutton, A. , Rand, 1965.   ICB-2

HUTCHINSON, William M.   1916-

He was born in Norfolk, Virginia and spent his childhood
in Virginia and West Virginia.   He studied at Cleveland
Art Institute in Ohio and has been a free-lance artist.
Mr. Hutchinson has made his home in Westport, Connec-
ticut.   For young people he illustrated: Latin American
Tales: From the Pampas to the Pyramids of Mexico,
Barlow, G. , Rand, 1967; The Promised Year, Uchida,
Y. , Harcourt, 1959.   ICB-3

HYMAN, Trina Schart   1939-

She was born in Philadelphia, Pennsylvania and attended
the College of Art there.   She also studied in Boston at
the Museum School and in Sweden at Stockholm's Kon-
stfackskolan.   After her marriage in 1959 to engineer
and mathematician Harris Hyman, she lived in Sweden
and Boston, Massachusetts before moving to New York.
Juvenile stories which she illustrated include: All In
Free But Janey, Johnson, E. , Little, 1968; George,
Turnbull, A. , Houghton, 1965; Joy To The World, Sawyer,
R. , Little, 1966.   ICB-3

ILSLEY, Velma Elizabeth   1918-

She was born in Edmonton, Alberta, Canada and later
made her home in New York City.   At one time she lived
in California, Florida, New Jersey, and Nova Scotia.

She received her education at Douglass College in New
Brunswick, New Jersey and at the Moore Institute of Art,
Science and Industry in Philadelphia. She also studied
at the Art Students League in New York. Velma Ilsley
has been a fashion illustrator and portrait painter in addition to book illustrator. Her work includes Kate And
The Apple Tree, Agle, N. , Seabury, 1965. She also
wrote and illustrated: Busy Day For Chris, Lippincott,
1957; The Long Stocking, Lippincott, 1959.   ICB-2

JACQUES, Faith

British artist and lecturer, born in Leicester, England.
She completed her education at London's Central School
of Arts and Crafts after serving with the Women's Royal
Naval Service during World War II. Miss Jacques has
lectured at art schools in Surrey and London where she
has made her home. She illustrated The Windswept City
(A Junior Literary Guild selection), Treece, H. , Meredith, 1968.

JACQUES, Robin   1920-

Born in Chelsea, London, he has traveled and lived in
Africa, Mexico, and the United States. The Jacques
family later moved to the south of France. In addition
to book illustration, Robin Jacques has worked in advertising and was the Art Editor of a magazine. He
served in the British Army during World War II and has
been a Fellow of the British Society of Industrial Artists.
For boys and girls he illustrated: Black Hearts in
Battersea (A Junior Literary Guild selection), Aiken,
J. , Doubleday, 1964; The Flood at Reedsmere, Burton,

Jefferson, Robert Louis 1929-
    H. , World, 1968; Nightbirds On Nantucket (A Junior Lit-
    erary Guild selection), Aiken, J. , Doubleday, 1966.

                                            ICB-2, ICB-3

JEFFERSON, Robert Louis 1929-
    Native Pennsylvanian, he has made his home in Phila-
    delphia. He also lived in Morocco for two years. The
    artist studied in Paris at the Academie de la Grande
    Chaumiére and the Sorbonne after attending Philadelphia's
    Museum College of Art. For boys and girls he illustra-
    ted: Run Away, Habeeb!, Cretan, G. , Abingdon Press,
    1968; Susan And Jane Learn To Ride, Self, M. , Macrae
    Smith, 1965.

JOHNSON, John E. 1929-
    Born in Worcester, Massachusetts, he studied at the
    Philadelphia College of Art. Following service in the
    army, he worked for a greeting card company in New
    York. In addition to illustrating books, he has drawn
    for magazines and worked in advertising. He married
    an artist and has lived in New York City. His work in-
    cludes: Beef Stew, Brenner, B. , Knopf, 1965; Just
    Around The Corner, Jacobs, L. , Holt, 1964.   ICB-3

JONES, Elizabeth Orton 1910-
    Author-illustrator, born in Highland Park, Illinois. She
    studied art at the University of Chicago, and has studied
    painting at Fontainebleau and in Paris. Elizabeth Orton
    Jones has illustrated many books for various authors.
    In 1945 she received the Caldecott Medal for Prayer For
    A Child (Macmillan, 1944) written by Rachel Field. She

has had a studio in Highland Park, Illinois and has lived
in Mason, New Hampshire.   She has illustrated some
books written by her mother, Jessie Mae (Orton) Jones
including: Secrets, Viking, 1945; This Is The Way,
Viking, 1951.   (Authors Of Books For Young People-
1964)   ICB-1, ICB-2

JONES, Harold 1904-

He was born in London and studied at St. Dunstan's
College and at the Royal College of Art.   During World
War II, he served with the Royal Engineers.   He collaborated with Walter de la Mare on his first book for
children.   His work has been acquired by the Victoria
and Albert Museum and the Tate Gallery.   The artist
has made his home in Putney, London.   He illustrated
Bless This Day, Vipont, E. , comp. Harcourt, 1958.

                                    ICB-1, ICB-2, ICB-3

JUCKER, Sita

She has been an illustrator for Elle (French woman's
magazine) and illustrated textbooks for boys and girls
in Switzerland.   Mrs. Jucker has also illustrated book
jackets and books in Geneva, Basel, and Paris.   For
young people she illustrated Squaps, Ziegler, U. , Atheneum, 1969.

KALMENOFF, Matthew

Born in New York City, he has been on the staff of the
American Museum of Natural History in New York.   His
work has appeared in many magazines including Natural
History and Audubon Magazine.   He has also painted

Karasz, Ilonka 1896-

backgrounds for habitat groups in many museums throughout the United States. The artist and his family have
lived in Scarsdale, New York. For young people he illustrated Animal Camouflage, Shuttlesworth, D. , Natural
History Press, 1966.

KARASZ, Ilonka 1896-
She was born in Hungary and studied at the Royal School
of Arts and Crafts in Budapest. In 1913 she came to the
United States where she has made her home with the ex-
ception of several years spent in Java, the Dutch East
Indies and Europe. Miss Karasz has designed covers
for the New Yorker magazine, textiles, china, and wallpaper. Her home has been in Brewster, New York. In
1949 the American Institute of Graphic Arts selected her
book The Twelve Days Of Christmas (Harper, 1949) as
one of the "Fifty Books of the Year." She also illustrated The Heavenly Tenants, Maxwell, W. , Harper, 1946.
                                                    ICB-2

KASHIWAGI, Isami 1925-
He was born in Onomea, Hawaii, attended the University
of Hawaii, Pennsylvania Academy of the Fine Arts, and
studied in Europe on a Cresson Traveling Scholarship.
His home has been in New York City. Isami (Sam)
Kashiwagi served as an interpreter with the occupation
forces in Japan. For young people he illustrated Hawai-
ian Treasure, Oakes, V. , Messner, 1957.   ICB-2

KAUFMANN, John 1931-
A native of New York, the artist has lived on Long Is-

land. He received his education in Philadelphia at the
Pennsylvania Academy of Fine Arts and in New York at
the Art Students League. He also studied in Florence,
Italy at the Instituto Statale D'Arte. At one time he
worked in an aircraft factory and also did technical illustration. Mr. Kaufmann has enjoyed bird watching as a
hobby and has painted watercolors of shore birds. For
boys and girls he illustrated: Animals As Parents, Selsam, M. , Morrow, 1965; Old Abe: the Eagle Hero
(A Junior Literary Guild selection), Young, P. , Prentice-
Hall, 1965.   ICB-3

KEATS, Ezra Jack 1916-

Illustrator-author, born in Brooklyn, New York. During
World War II, he was a camouflage expert in the United
States Air Corps. He has illustrated many books for
children, but The Snowy Day (Viking, 1962) was the first
book which Mr. Keats wrote and illustrated. It was this
book which won the Caldecott Medal in 1963. With Pat
Cherr he wrote My Dog Is Lost!, Crowell, 1960, and
he wrote and illustrated Peter's Chair, Harper, 1967.
(Authors Of Books For Young People-1964) ICB-2, ICB-3

KEEPING, Charles 1924-

Born in London, he later studied art there at the Polytechnic. He married painter Renate Meyer and has made
his home in Bromley, South London. Charles Keeping
served as a telegraph operator with the Royal Navy during World War II. Following the war, he did further
study in art on a full-time grant. His work has been exhibited in Australia, England, Italy, and the United States.

Mr. Keeping has been on the staff at Croydon College of Art and the Polytechnic. His illustrations have appeared in: The Apple Stone (A Junior Literary Guild selection), Gray, N., Meredith, 1969; Mainly In Moonlight (A Junior Literary Guild selection), Gray, N., 1967. He also wrote and illustrated Charley, Charlotte, and the Golden Canary, Watts, 1967.   ICB-3

KEITH, Eros

Resident of New York City, he studied at the University of Chicago and the Chicago Art Institute. Mr. Keith has worked in advertising, drawn covers for records and jackets for books, and his illustrations have also appeared in magazines. For young people he illustrated Ivanov Seven, Janeway, E., Harper, 1967.

KELLY, Walt 1913-

Cartoonist Walter Crawford Kelly was born in Philadelphia. He originated the character "Pogo" which has appeared in many newspapers. In 1951 he received the "Reuben" award from the National Cartoonists Society as "Cartoonist of the Year." Prior to being an editorial cartoonist on the New York Star, he was an animator in the Walt Disney Studios. His work includes: Complete Nursery Song Book, Bertail, I., ed., Lothrop, 1947; The Glob, O'Reilly, J., Viking, 1952.

KENT, Rockwell 1882-

He was born in Tarrytown Heights, New York and later studied at Columbia University. He has created lithographs and wood engravings in addition to painting and

drawing pictures.   Mr. Kent has also been a dairy farm-
er in New York state.   At one time he lived in Ireland,
Alaska, Greenland, and Newfoundland.   His work has
been included in the collections at the Metropolitan museum of Art in New York City and the Chicago Art Institute.   He illustrated Complete Works, Shakespeare,
W. (The Cambridge ed.), Garden City, 1936:   He wrote
and illustrated Wilderness, Halcyon, 1937.   ICB-1

KIDDELL-Monroe, Joan   1908-
Born in England, she studied at Willesden and Chelsea
School of Art.   Prior to becoming a freelance artist,
she worked in advertising.   She married Canadian artist
Webster Murray who died in 1951.   She has lived in
Mallorca.   She illustrated Welsh Legends And Folk-Tales,
Jones, G. (retold by), Oxford, 1955.   ICB-2, ICB-3

KIRMSE, Marguerite   1885-1954
She was born in Bournemouth, England.   She attended
London's Royal Academy School of Music, the Polytechnic School of Art, and Frank Calderon's School of Animal
Painting.   She came to the United States in 1910 as a
harpist in an orchestra.   She married George W. Cole
and lived on a farm in Bridgewater, Connecticut where
she and her husband kept dog kennels and raised blue-
ribbon winners.   For young readers she illustrated:
Nipper, the Little Bull Pup, L'Hommedieu, D., Lippincott, 1943; Togo, the Little Husky, L'Hommedieu, D.,
Lippincott, 1951.   ICB-1, ICB-2

KOCSIS, James C.   1936-

His pseudonym is James Paul.   Born in Buffalo, New
York, he grew up in Bethlehem, Pennsylvania, and later
made his home in Philadelphia.   He studied at the Fleis-
her Art Memorial School and attended the Philadelphia
College of Art on a scholarship.   He has been a member
of the Philadelphia College of Art faculty since 1965.
His career as a painter and illustrator began at the age
of fourteen when he held his first one-man show.   After
his discharge from the Army in World War II, James
Kocsis has been both a magazine and book illustrator.
His work for children includes: Edge Of Two Worlds,
Jones, W. , Dial, 1968; Trouble On Heron's Neck, Ladd,
E. , Morrow, 1966.   ICB-3

KOERING, Ursula   1921-

Born in Vineland, New Jersey, she spent part of her
childhood in Indiana and New Jersey.   She studied at the
Philadelphia Museum School of Art.   In addition to illustrating books, she has enjoyed sculpturing and working
in pottery.   Her work includes: Picture Story Of Denmark, O'Neill, H. , McKay, 1952; Picture Story Of Norway, O'Neill, H. , McKay, 1951; Mystery At Squaw Peak,
Hayes, W. , Atheneum, 1965.   ICB-2

KRAUSS, Oscar

New York art director.   He has been associated with the
National Society of Art Directors and the Art Directors
Club.   Prior to studying art and design at Pratt Institute,
he was interested in architecture.   He designed: The
Art Of Ancient Greece, Glubok, S. , Atheneum, 1963;

Kredel, Fritz 1900-
The Art Of Ancient Rome, Glubok, S. , Harper, 1965.

KREDEL, Fritz 1900-

Artist and teacher, born in Michelstadt, Odenwald, Germany. He attended art school in Offenbach-am-Main at
Kunstgewerbeschule. He became an American citizen
after coming to the United States in 1938 and has lived
in New York City. At one time Mr. Kredel taught art
in Germany and later served on the staff at Cooper Union
Art School in New York. He has received many honors
for his work including the 1938 Golden Medal for Book
Illustration in Paris, and the 1960 Goethe Plaquette in
Germany. He was also awarded the Silver Jubilee Cita-
tion of the Limited Editions Club in 1954. For children
he illustrated: The King Of the Golden River, Ruskin,
J. , World, 1946; Little Town Of Bethlehem, Pauli, H. ,
Duell, 1963.   ICB-1, ICB-2, ICB-3

KRUSH, Joe 1918-   Beth 1918-

Husband-wife team. He was born in Camden, New Jersey, and she was born in Washington, D.C. Both attended the Museum School of Art in Philadelphia, and both
have been art instructors. He served with the Office
of Strategic Services during World War II. The Krushs
have lived in Wayne, Pennsylvania and have enjoyed
model airplanes and tennis as special interests. They
have been the recipients of many awards for drawing and
water color. Together they illustrated Magic To Burn,
Fritz, J. , Coward, 1964.   ICB-2, ICB-3

KUBINYI, Laszlo

The artist grew up in Massachusetts on Cape Ann. He
has traveled in the Middle East and throughout the world.
His home has been in New York City. Mr. Kubinyi received his education in Massachusetts at the Boston Museum School and in New York at the Art Students League.
He also attended the School of Visual Arts. In addition
to book illustration, he has played the dumbek (a Middle
Eastern drum) in an Armenian orchestra. For boys and
girls he illustrated Perplexing Puzzles And Tantalizing
Teasers, Gardner, M. , Simon, 1969.

LAITE, Gordon 1925-

He was born in New York City and studied at Beloit
College in Beloit, Wisconsin and at the Chicago Art In-
stitute. He was raised by Charles and Blanche Fisher
Laite who illustrated The Real Mother Goose (Rand, 1916)
under the name of Blanche Fisher Wright. Gordon Laite
and his wife Jeanne and two children have lived in Gal-
lup, New Mexico since 1962. His work includes: ...
Elves and Ellefolk, Belting, N. , Holt, 1961; Religions
Around the World, Wolcott, L. , Abingdon, 1967; Stories
From India, Dolch, E. , Garrard, 1961.   ICB-3

LAMBO, Don

Graduate of Princeton University, he studied art at Pratt
Institute. He has worked in advertising in addition to
illustrating books for young people. Mr. Lambo's interests have included photography and woodworking. On his
travels around the world he took many photographs which
helped him illustrate: Getting To Know The Soviet Union,

Landau, Jacob 1917-
Wallace, J., Coward-McCann, 1964; Getting To Know
The U.S.S.R., Wallace, J., Coward-McCann, 1959. He
also illustrated Jared and the Yankee Genius, Crary, M.,
McKay, 1965.

LANDAU, Jacob 1917-
Artist, photographer, teacher. Born in Philadelphia,
Pennsylvania, he has lived in Roosevelt, New Jersey. He
studied at Philadelphia's Museum School of Art, New
York's New School for Research, and France's Académie
de la Grande Chaumière in Paris. He served with the
Special Services, Engineer Command, during World War
II. In addition to illustrating books, Mr. Landau has
worked in advertising and produced film strips for the
United Nations Secretariat. He has also been a photog-
rapher and editor and has been on the staff at the Phil-
adelphia Museum School of Art and Pratt Institute in
Brooklyn. His work has been exhibited both here and
abroad. He has received many honors including the 1967
National Arts Endowment Grant. For young readers he
illustrated The Wright Brothers, Pioneers Of American
Aviation, Reynolds, Q., Random, 1950. ICB-2, ICB-3

LANGNER, Nola 1930
Born in New York City, she attended Bennington College
and also studied art at the Yale School of Fine Arts.
She began her career working for a magazine and in a
television art studio. Married to a sociologist, she has
lived in New York City. Her work for young people includes: How To Catch A Crocodile, Pack, R., Knopf,
1964; Who Has A Secret?, McGovern, A., Houghton,

LATHROP, Dorothy Pulis 1891-
Illustrator, author, teacher, born in Albany, New York.
She attended Teachers College, Columbia University,
Pennsylvania Academy of Fine Arts, and the Art Students
League. Mrs. Lathrop has illustrated many books by
different authors and in 1938 she received the first
Caldecott Medal for the illustrations in Animals Of The
Bible (Stokes, 1937). She has lived in Albany, New York.
Other titles include: Angel In The Woods, Macmillan,
1947; Follow The Brook, Macmillan, 1960; Let Them
Live, Macmillan, 1951; Littlest Mouse, Macmillan, 1955;
Presents For Lupe, Macmillan, 1940; Puppies For
Keeps, Macmillan, 1943; Who Goes There?, Macmillan,
1935. (Authors Of Books For Young People-1964)
ICB-1, ICB-2, ICB-3

LAURENCE
Designer and illustrator. This French artist began her
career in Paris where she also attended school. She
was awarded a French government cultural fellowship
for her work in 1964. The artist lived in New York
City while her husband attended Columbia University.
She wrote and illustrated A Village In Normandy, Bobbs,
1968.

LAWRENCE, Jacob
Born in Atlantic City, New Jersey, he studied at the
Harlem Workshop and the American Artists School.
Recipient of both the Rosenwald and Guggenheim fellow-

ships, Mr. Lawrence has been Artist in Residence at
Brandeis University. He has also served on the staff
of Pratt Institute, the Art Students League, and the New
School for Social Research. His work has been repre-
sented in many permanent museum collections including:
the Metropolitan Museum of Art, the Whitney Museum,
and the Museum of Modern Art. For boys and girls he
wrote and illustrated Harriet and the Promised Land,
Simon, 1968.

LAWSON, Robert 1892-1957
Native New Yorker. He attended school in Montclair,
New Jersey and received training in art at the New York
School of Fine and Applied Art. During World War I,
he served in the Camouflage Section of the United States
Army in France. He has lived near Westport, Connecti-
cut in a house called "Rabbit Hill." He was awarded the
Newbery Medal in 1945 for his book, Rabbit Hill, Viking,
1944. Juvenile contributions include: Ben And Me,
Little, 1939; Fabulous Flight, Little, 1949; Great Wheel,
Viking, 1957; I Discover Columbus, Little, 1941; Mr.
Revere And I, Little, 1953. In 1941 he was awarded the
Caldecott Medal for They Were Strong And Good, Viking,
1940. (Authors Of Books For Young People-1964)

                                        ICB-1, ICB-2

LAZARE, Gerald John 1927-
Jerry Lazare was born in Toronto, Ontario, Canada.
He studied at Oakwood Collegiate and took Famous Artists
Course. During World War II, he did comic strips.
Following the war, he studied in Paris and London. He

Lee, Manning De Villeneuve 1894-

has worked in advertising and has illustrated for mag-
azines. For young people he illustrated: Queenie
Peavy, Burch, R., Viking, 1966; Take Wing (A Junior
Literary Guild selection), Little, J., Little, 1968.

                                                    ICB-3

LEE, Manning De Villeneuve   1894-
   Artist, illustrator, art instructor, born in Summerville,
South Carolina. He grew up in South Carolina and
Georgia. He later made his home in Ambler, Pennsyl-
vania. He received his education at the Porter Military
Academy, Pennsylvania Academy of the Fine Arts, and
the Fine Arts School in Saumur, France. After serving
as an artillery officer in World War I, he continued his
studies in Europe on an Academy Traveling Scholarship.
The recipient of many awards, Manning Lee has belonged
to the Philadelphia Art Alliance, Southern States Art
League, and was elected a Fellow of London's Royal
Society of Arts. Mr. Manning has conducted art classes,
designed postage stamps, and religious film strips. His
book illustrations include: Bible Stories, Jones, M.,
Rand, 1952; Things To Do, Lee, T. Doubleday, 1965.

                                                ICB-1, ICB-2

LEICHMAN, Seymour
   Native of New York, he studied at New York's Cooper
Union. Prior to a career as a painter, Mr. Leichman
worked in the advertising field. His paintings have been
exhibited in this country and Mexico. He has also been
interested in murals (a thirty foot outdoor mural in
Kingston, Jamaica) and motion pictures. For young

people he wrote and illustrated The Boy Who Could Sing
Pictures (A Junior Literary Guild selection), Doubleday,
1968.

LEIGHT, Edward

After graduating from the Parsons School of Design,
Edward Leight taught painting to children. He has also
designed theater sets, wallpapers, and textiles. He served with the Armed Forces during World War II and
after the war exhibited his overseas paintings in this
country. Mr. Leight has enjoyed cooking and the theater
as special interests. He collaborated with Nancy Moore
to write Miss Harriet Hippopotamus And the Most Wonderful, Vanguard, 1963. He also illustrated Nancy
Moore's book Ermintrude, Vanguard, 1960.

LEMKE, Horst 1922-

Artist, cartoonist, painter. Born in Berlin, Germany,
he studied there at the Staatliche Hocheschule. He also
attended the High School of Plastic Arts. He moved to
Heidelberg after World War II. Since 1955, he has
lived in Switzerland. For boys and girls he illustrated
Jan And The Wild Horse, Denneborg, H., McKay, 1958.
                                                    ICB-3

LENT, Blair 1930-

He was born in Boston, Massachusetts and attended the
Boston Museum School and also studied in Europe on a
Cummings Traveling Scholarship. He illustrated The
Wave (Hodges, M., Houghton, 1964) which was runner-
up for the Caldecott Medal in 1965. He has made his

Lippman, Peter J. 1936-
home in Cambridge, Massachusetts. He also illustrated
The Christmas Sky, Branley, F., Crowell, 1966. ICB-3

LIPPMAN, Peter J. 1936-
He was born in Flushing, New York and graduated from
Columbia College and the Columbia School of Architecture.
He also studied at the Art Students League. His drawings have appeared in Holiday magazine, and he has
written articles on the history of architecture. He wrote
and illustrated Plunkety Plunk, Ariel, 1963. He also
illustrated Sparrow Socks, Selden, G., Harper, 1965.
ICB-3

LOBEL, Anita 1934-
Artist and textile designer. Born in Cracow, Poland, she
grew up in Poland and Sweden and later studied at Pratt
Institute in Brooklyn, New York. Her husband Arnold
Lobel has also been an illustrator and author of books
for boys and girls. They have lived in Brooklyn, New
York. She wrote and illustrated: Potatoes, Potatoes,
Harper, 1967; The Troll Music, Harper, 1966. She also
illustrated: Indian Summer, Monjo, F., Harper, 1968;
Puppy Summer, DeJong, M., Harper, 1966. ICB-3

LOEWENSTEIN, Bernice
She was born in New York City, attended the Art Students
League, and graduated from Bryn Mawr College in Pennsylvania. Mrs. Loewenstein and her family have made
their home in Binghamton, New York. At one time the
illustrator was associated with publishing firms where
she worked in the children's book departments. For

Lorraine, Walter Henry 1929-   71

young readers she illustrated <u>Bess and the Sphinx</u>, Coatsworth, E. , Macmillan, 1967.

LORRAINE, Walter Henry 1929-
Born in Worcester, Massachusetts, he later made his
home in Newton. Walter Lorraine graduated from the
Rhode Island School of Design in Providence after two
years spent in the Navy. He worked as a book designer
and production head in a publishing firm before he became an illustrator of books. He has also been on the
staff at the Museum of Fine Arts School and Boston
University. His illustrations in Alastair Reid's <u>I Will</u>
<u>Tell You Of a Town</u> (Houghton, 1956) and in Julia Cun-
ningham's <u>Dear Rat</u> (Houghton, 1961) were among the "Ten
Best illustrated Children's Books" in 1956 and 1961 selected by the <u>New York Times</u>. Other juvenile books which
he illustrated include: <u>The Dog Who Thought He Was a</u>
<u>Boy</u>, Annett, C. , Houghton, 1965; <u>From Ambledee To</u>
<u>Zumbledee</u>, Warburg, S. , Houghton, 1968. ICB-2, ICB-3

LUDWIG, Helen
She studied at the Hartford, Connecticut Art School and
the Art Students' League in New York. Later she and
her husband, a philosophy professor, made their home in
San Francisco. Her work has appeared in galleries, and
she has had one-man shows. For young people she illustrated <u>All About Eggs</u>, Selsam, M. , Scott. 1952.

MCCAFFERY, Janet
She graduated from the Philadelphia College of Art.
Prior to her marriage, she worked at Street and Smith

Publications.   Later she worked as a free lance artist
in advertising and in both book and magazine illustration.
She has lived in New York City.   Her work includes:
The Goblin Under The Stairs, Calhoun, M. , Morrow,
1968; The Last Two Elves In Denmark, Calhoun, M. ,
Morrow, 1968; Mrs. Popover Goes To The Zoo. Everson,
D. , Morrow, 1963.

MCCLOSKEY, Robert 1914-
Born in Hamilton, Ohio, he studied at the National Academy of Design in New York.   During World War II, he
was in the Army where he drew training pictures.   He
has been the recipient of several awards including the
Prix de Rome in 1939, and the Caldecott Medal in 1942
and again in 1958.   The award in 1942 was given to him
for his book Make Way For Ducklings (Viking, 1941) and
in 1958 for his book Time Of Wonder (Viking, 1957).
The McCloskey family has lived on an island off the
coast of Maine.   His titles include: Blueberries For Sal,
Viking, 1948; Centerburg Tales, Viking, 1951; Homer
Price, Viking, 1943; Lentil, Viking, 1940; One Morning
In Maine, Viking, 1952.   (Authors Of Books For Young
People-1964)   ICB-1,   ICB-2,   ICB-3

MCCULLY, Emily Arnold 1939-
Born in Galesburg, Illinois, she graduated from Brown
University and received an M.A. degree in Art History
from Columbia.   At one time she lived in Brussels and
New York but later made her home in Swarthmore, Penn-
sylvania where her husband has been a professor of
Renaissance and Reformation history at Swarthmore

College.   Mrs. McCully has designed book jackets in
addition to book illustrations.   Her work has also appeared in magazines.   For young readers she illustrated:
Luigi Of the Streets, Carlson, N. , Harper, 1967; Sea
Beach Express,   Panetta, G. , Harper, 1966; The Seven-
teenth-Street Gang, Neville, E. , Harper, 1966.   ICB-3

MACDONALD, James
Born in Scotland, he later lived in Roslyn, New York.
He studied art in both Scotland and the United States.   He
has worked in advertising in addition to illustrating books
and book jackets, maps, and title pages.   Mr. MacDonald
has enjoyed travel and painting (water colors) in Maine.
For young people he illustrated Davy Crockett, Rourke,
C. , Harcourt, 1934.

MCINTYRE, Kevin
Born in New York City, he graduated from Syracuse University.   In 1969-70 he was awarded a Fine Arts Fellowship to study in Florence, Italy.   When he was twenty-
one, he illustrated his first book, and his fourth one was
The Wild And Free, Devlin, T. , Scribner, 1969.

MACKAY, Donald A.
Artist, illustrator, painter.   His home has been in
Ossining, New York.   The American Watercolor Society
and the Society of Illustrators have exhibited his pictures.
His work has also appeared in such magazines as Harper's, Life, and Newsweek.   For boys and girls he illustrated The Stone-Faced Boy, Fox, P. , Bradbury Press,
1969.

MACKENZIE, Garry 1921-

Born in Manitoba, Canada, he studied in Los Angeles at
Chouinard Art Institute. In 1945 he went to New York
City and began illustrating children's books. Following
a stay in Cambridge, England, he lived on Staten Island,
New York. His work includes: Flickertail, Bailey, C.,
Walck, 1962; Here Come The Cottontails!, Goudey, A.,
Scribner, 1965.   ICB-2, ICB-3

MACKNIGHT, Ninon 1908-

Ninon is her pseudonym. She was born and raised in
Sydney, Australia. Later she came to the United States
and began illustrating books for boys and girls. She
married Wilbur Jordan Smith and has lived in Woodland
Hills, California. Her work includes: For A Child,
McFarland, W., ed., Junior Literary Guild and Westminster, 1947; Scaredy Cat, Krasilovsky, P., Macmillan,
1959.   ICB-2

MCLACHLIN, Steve

Illustrator-painter. Mr. McLachlin and his family have
made their home in Ormand Beach, Florida. He combined his work as an artist with his love of animals to
illustrate a book for boys and girls entitled Dear Prosper,
Fox, P., David White, 1968.

MCMULLAN, James 1934-

He was born in Tsingtao, North China, grew up in China,
Canada, and India, and came to the United States in 1951.
His home has been in New York City since 1959 when he
became an American citizen. He studied art in Seattle

and at Pratt Institute in Brooklyn. Mr. McMullan has
been honored by the American Institute of Graphic Arts
and the Society of Illustrators. He also received recognition from <u>Print</u> magazine. The artist has been associated with the Push Pin Studios since 1964. In addition
to book illustration, he has worked in advertising and designed book jackets. For boys and girls he illustrated:
<u>Kangaroo & Kangaroo</u>, Braun, K. , Doubleday, 1965; <u>The
Last Little Cat</u>, De Jong, M. , Harper, 1961.   ICB-3

MCNAUGHT, Harry

Born in Scotland, he grew up in Philadelphia. He studied
at the Philadelphia Museum School of Art. He later lived
with his wife and four children in Carversville, Pennsylvania. He illustrated <u>The Land, Wildlife, And Peoples
Of The Bible</u>, Farb, P. , Harper, 1967.

MAAS, Julie

A native New Yorker, she has lived on New York's lower
east side since her marriage to photographer Michael
Shields. She received her early education in art from her
parents who were both artists. Julie Maas began her
career as a book illustrator after graduating from high
school. Juvenile books which she has illustrated include:
<u>Apple Vendor's Fair</u>, Hubbell, P. , Atheneum, 1963; <u>8
A. M. Shadows</u>, Hubbell, P. , Atheneum, 1965; <u>"It's
Spring," She Said,</u> Blos, J. , Knopf, 1968.

MALVERN, Corinne

Sister of author Gladys Malvern, she studied for four
years at the Art Students League in New York. She later

lived in Los Angeles where she drew fashion advertisements and continued her art studies at night.   She has
had one man shows and for boys and girls she illustrated: Eric's Girls, Malvern, G. , Messner, 1949; The
Foreigner (A Junior Literary Guild selection), Malvern,
G. , Longmans, 1954; Your Kind Indulgence, Malvern,
G. , Messner, 1948.

MAROKVIA, Artur   1909-

He was born in Stuttgart, Germany where he later studied
painting at the Akademie and at the Académie de la
Grande Chaumière in Paris.   He also received a diploma
from the School of Music in Dresden.   He has painted in
Greece, Austria, Mexico, Yugoslavia, Finland, Russia,
and Spain.   His favorite hobby has been playing the piano.
He and his wife have lived in New York City and Cuern-
avaca, Mexico.   He illustrated in four colors When In-
sects Are Babies (A Junior Literary Guild selection),
Conklin, G. , Holiday, 1969.   ICB-2, ICB-3

MARS, Witold T.   1908-

He was born and grew up in Poland and received his
early education in the schools of Cracow.   After graduating from the Academy of Fine Arts in Warsaw, Poland,
he continued to study art in Italy, France, and Germany.
He served with the Polish Forces in Great Britain during World War II.   After the war, Mr. Mars exhibited
his paintings in many galleries throughout England and
also did book illustrations for several British publishers.
He came to the United States in 1951 and has lived in
Forest Hills, Long Island.   He has been a member of

New York's Polish Institute of Art and Science since
1965. For boys and girls he illustrated: Andy Buckram's
Tin Men (A Junior Literary Guild selection), Brink, C.,
Viking, 1966; Fairy Tales From Viet Nam, retold by
Robertson, D., Dodd, 1968.   ICB-2, ICB-3

MARSH, Reginald 1898-1954
Born in Paris, France, he came to America at an early
age and grew up in New Jersey. A Yale University graduate, he also studied at New York's Art Students League
and in Europe. His illustrations and sketches have appeared in magazines and newspapers. Mr. Marsh has
been an art instructor at Moore Institute and the Art
Students League and has also designed for the theater.
His paintings can be found in the permanent collections
of the Library of Congress, Metropolitan Museum of Art,
and Whitney Museum. He has been the recipient of many
art awards. For boys and girls he illustrated The Story
of a Bad Boy, Aldrich, T., Pantheon, 1951.   ICB-2

MARTIN, David Stone 1913-
He was born in Chicago, Illinois, the son of a Presby-
terian minister. He later lived in California and New
York. He studied at the Chicago Art Institute. He began
his career as an artist at the Chicago World's Fair in
1933 when he served as an architect's assistant. He later
became head of the Federal Arts Project in Chicago and
was artist correspondent for Life magazine during World
War II. In addition to book and magazine illustration,
Mr. Martin has designed jazz album covers and worked
in commercial advertising. He has also been an art

director.   His work has been exhibited at galleries and
museums throughout this country.   David Martin has been
honored many times by the Art Directors Club of New
York and the Society of Illustrators.   For young people
he illustrated Journey Into Jazz, Hentoff, N. , Coward,
1968.   ICB-2

MARTIN, René
He was born in Paris, the son of an engraver and artist.
He studied art in Switzerland and received several fine
arts grants from the Swiss government.   At one time Mr.
Martin lived and painted in Morocco.   He became an
American citizen and made his home in Key Largo, Florida.   His work includes: All About The Weather, Tan-
nehill, I. , Random, 1953; Blood, Zim, H. , Morrow,
1968.

MARTIN, Stefan 1936-
Artist and wood engraver, born in Elgin, Illinois.   He
grew up in New York and New Jersey and studied at
Chicago's Art Institute.   He has been on the staff of the
Art Center in Summit, New Jersey and has resided in
Roosevelt, New Jersey.   Mr. Martin's work can be found
in private collections, and he was awarded the Tiffany
Grant in print-making.   He has also been honored for
his book illustrations for children.   His work includes
They Walk In The Night, Coatsworth, E. , Norton, 1969.
                                                            ICB-3

MARTINEZ, John
He was born in New York City and studied at the Art

Students League and the School of Visual Arts. In addition to illustrating books, he has also been a painter. Mr. Martinez has lived in Leonardtown, Maryland. For boys and girls he illustrated Hidden Year Of Devlin Bates, Muehl, L., Holiday, 1967.

MATULAY, Laszlo 1912-

Born in Vienna, Austria where he attended the Academy of Applied Arts. He also studied in New York at the New School for Social Research after coming to the United States in 1935. He has lived in Hampton and Flemington, New Jersey. Mr. Matulay served in the U. S. Army during World War II. In addition to books, he has illustrated for magazines and has been an art director. For children he illustrated Discovery By Chance, Batten, M., Funk, 1968. ICB-2

MAXEY, Betty

She spent her childhood in Chicago where she attended the Chicago Art Institute and the American Academy of Art. Mrs. Maxey has worked in advertising in New York, Chicago, and London. She has also created book jackets and illustrations for magazines. Her husband Dale has been both an author and illustrator. Her work includes The Family At Caldicott Place (A Junior Literary Guild selection), Streatfeild, N., Random, 1968.

MAYER, Mercer 1943-

He was born in Little Rock, Arkansas, spent his childhood in Hawaii, and later lived in Sea Cliff, Long Island. Prior to devoting full-time to book illustration, he was

an art director in an advertising agency.   He wrote and
illustrated There's A Nightmare In My Closet, Dial, 1968.
He also illustrated The Gillygoofang, Mendoza, G., Dial,
1968.

MERKLING, Erica

Artist-teacher.   Born in Vienna, she later made her
home in New York City with her husband and children.
Prior to book illustration, Erica Merkling was a fashion
designer and an art instructor at Parsons School of Design.   For children she illustrated The Best Place,
Schlein, M., Whitman, 1968.

MERWIN, Decie 1894-

Born in Middlesboro, Kentucky, she grew up in Tenn-
essee, and later lived in New York City following her
marriage to writer Jack Bechdolt.   She attended boarding
school in Cincinnati, Ohio and art school in Boston,
Massachusetts.   Her work has appeared in The Christian
Science Monitor.   For young readers she illustrated:
Fairies And Suchlike, Eastwick, I., Dutton, 1946; Wise
House, Palmer, R., Harper, 1951.   ICB-2

MICOLEAU, Tyler

Artist, professional ski instructor, graduate of the Rhode
Island School of Design.   He has been a commercial
artist and has been an art instructor at Brown University.
He has also taught skiing in Jackson, New Hampshire
and at Squaw Valley, California.   He designed and illustrated Tennis Techniques Illustrated, Mace, W., Barnes,
1952.

MILHOUS, Katherine 1894-

Illustrator, author, native of Philadelphia. She attended the Pennsylvania Museum's School of Industrial Art and the Academy of Fine Arts. She was the recipient of a Cresson traveling scholarship and studied abroad. Miss Milhous has served as supervisor on a Federal Art Project. Many of her stories have had a Pennsylvania Dutch background. She received the Caldecott Medal in 1951 for The Egg Tree, Scribner, 1950. Other titles include: Appolonia's Valentine, Junior Literary Guild and Scribner, 1954; First Christmas Crib, Scribner, 1944; Herodia, The Lovely Puppet, Scribner, 1942; Patrick And The Golden Slippers, Junior Literary Guild and Scribner, 1951; With Bells On (A Junior Literary Guild selection), Scribner, 1955. (Authors Of Books For Young People-1964)   ICB-1, ICB-2, ICB-3

MILL, Eleanor

She was born in Detroit, Michigan and studied at the Corcoran School of Art in Washington, D.C. Both her mother and her husband have been artists. She has made her home in Rhinebeck, New York. Her illustrations for young people include: Getting to Know Indonesia, Taylor, C., Coward-McCann, 1961; What Mary Jo Shared, Udry, J., Whitman, 1966.

MINALE, Marcello 1938-

Born in Tripoli, Libya, Africa, he studied art in Naples, Italy. At one time he lived in Scandinavia and Finland and later worked in graphic design. In 1964 he became partners with Brian Tattersfield and formed a company called Minale, Tattersfield, Ltd. which has specialized

in design (both industrial and book design). For children
he illustrated Creatures Great and Small, Flanders, M.,
Holt, 1965.   ICB-3

MITSUHASHI, Yoko
Illustrator and designer, born in Tokyo, Japan. After
graduating from the Women's College of Fine Arts in
Tokyo, she became associated with Japan's leading studio
of design, the Nippon Design Center. She was one of
the few women chosen for membership in the Japan Advertising Artists Club. Her work has appeared in national magazines, and she has worked in New York since
1962. For boys and girls she illustrated I Have A Horse
Of My Own, Zolotow, C., Abelard-Schuman, 1964.

MITSUI, Eiichi
This Japanese artist has illustrated several of Betty
Jean Lifton's books for boys and girls. These include:
Joji And The Fog, Lifton, B., Morrow, 1959; Kap The
Kappa, Lifton, B., Morrow, 1960; The Rice-Cake Rab-
bit, Lifton, B., Norton, 1966.   ICB-3

MIZUMURA, Kazue
Artist-author, born in Kamakura, Japan. She studied
at Tokyo's Women's Art Institute and Pratt Institute in
Brooklyn, New York. Her husband Claus Stamm has
also been a writer. In addition to book illustration, she
has worked in advertising and textile design. Her home
has been in Stamford, Connecticut. She wrote and illustrated I See the Winds, Crowell, 1966. She also illustrated Chie and the Sports Day, Matsuno, M., World,

Mocniak, George

1965 and Algernon and the Pigeons, Plasmati, V., Viking,
1963.   ICB-3

MOCNIAK, George

He was born in Greensboro, Pennyslvania and studied at
the School of Industrial Art and the School of Visual Arts
in New York City.   At one time Mr. Mocniak lived in
Hamburg, Germany.   He later made his home in New
York City.   His work for young people includes painting
of book jackets for the following: Blood For Holly Warner,
Hample, S., Harper, 1967; The Contender, Lipsyte, R.,
Harper, 1967.   He also illustrated Traveler From A
Small Kingdom, Neville, E., Harper, 1968.

MONTRESOR, Beni 1926-

Designer, illustrator, born in Verona, Italy.   He attended
Verona Art School, the Academy of Fine Arts in Venice,
and was awarded a two-year scholarship to the Centro
Sperimentale di Cinematographia in Rome.   After his
arrival in the United States, he illustrated and wrote
picture books.   Also he designed the sets and costumes
for the Broadway musical "Do I Hear A Waltz?" and the
Metropolitan Opera productions of "The Last Savage" and
"Centerentola."   In 1965 he was awarded the Caldecott
Medal for his illustrations in May I Bring A Friend? (A
Junior Literary Guild selection), De Regniers, B.,
Atheneum, 1964.   He wrote and illustrated: House Of
Flowers, House Of Stars, Knopf, 1962; Witches Of Ven-
ice, Knopf, 1963.   (Authors Of Books For Young People-
1967)   ICB-3

MOORE, Janet Gaylord

Artist, painter, teacher. Miss Moore has lived in Cleveland, Ohio where she has been an Associate Curator at the Cleveland Museum of Art. Her summers have been spent in Maine on Deer Isle. She has been a teacher and lecturer on art. For young readers she wrote and illustrated The Many Ways Of Seeing, World, 1968.

MORAN, Connie

Mrs. Moran has lived in a studio apartment on Chicago's North Side. Her fondness for both dogs and cats resulted in her animal illustrations for books. Her work includes: Bow Wow! Said the Kittens, Meeks, E. , Wilcox, 1952; Steam Shovel Family, Eberle, I. , McKay, 1948.

MORDVINOFF, Nicolas 1911-

His pseudonym is Nicolas. Author, artist, born in Petrograd (now known as Leningrad). He graduated from the University of Paris. He began drawing at an early age and continued to do so when he lived in the South Pacific. In Tahiti writer William Stone asked him to illustrate a book which later influenced his coming to America. Bear's Land (Coward, 1955) was the first book written by Nicolas Mordvinoff. He collaborated with William Lipkind to write books for children. In 1952 this team, known as Will and Nicolas, won the Caldecott Medal for Finders Keepers (Illustrated by Mr. Mordvinoff), Harcourt, 1951. (Authors Of Books For Young People-1964)

ICB-1, ICB-2, ICB-3

MORROW, Barbara

She grew up in Cleveland Heights, Ohio. Her father used
to operate a print and antiques gallery in a Cleveland
bookstore. Mrs. Morrow studied mural painting at the
Cleveland Institute of Art. She has worked in an art library and has also been a college art instructor. Her
husband Robert has taught at Kent State University in
Kent, Ohio. The first children's book which she illustrated was Chicken Ten Thousand (A Junior Literary Guild
selection), Jackson, J., Little, 1968.

MORTON, Marian

Her husband has also been an artist, and they have lived
in Mamaroneck, New York. She has worked in graphics
and ceramic sculpture in addition to magazine and advertising illustration. Marian Morton studied art in South
America and Europe. She has illustrated adult books and
for young people illustrated Bo and the Old Donkey, Sand-
burg, H., Dial Press, 1965.

MOYERS, William 1916-

Artist, cowboy, teacher. Born in Atlanta, Georgia, he
grew up on a ranch in Colorado. After graduating from
Colorado's Adams State College in Alamosa he studied
at the Los Angeles Art Institute. When he was a young
man, Mr. Moyers rode in rodeos. He later became a
cartoonist at the Walt Disney Studio and was a high school
teacher. He served in the Army Signal Corps during
World War II. They Moyers family has lived in New
Mexico and Georgia. He illustrated Famous Indian Tribes
(Random House, 1954) which he co-authored with David C.

Cooke.   Juvenile books which he illustrated include:
Coming of the King, Peale, N. , Prentice-Hall, 1956;
Ten Gallon Hat, Garst, S. , Ariel Bks. , 1953.   ICB-2

MULLINS, Edward S.
He studied in Boston at the New England School of Art
and graduated from Boston University.   He has lived in
Connecticut where he has been an art instructor at Milford Academy.   Mr. Mullins has also conducted art
classes in his studio and designed greeting cards in addition to book illustrations.   He has also done portrait
painting.   He wrote and illustrated Animal Limericks,
Follett, 1966.

NADLER, Robert
Architect and artist, born in Alexandria, Egypt.   He received a degree in architecture from the University of
Pennsylvania in Philadelphia.   He married an architect
and has lived in New York.   Mr. Nadler has belonged
to the American Institute of Architects.   For young readers he illustrated The Iron Giant, Hughes, T. , Harper,
1968.

NAGY, Al
Designer-illustrator, born in New York City.   He studied
art at New York's Cooper Union.   Mr. Nagy has been a
commercial artist in addition to illustrating books.   For
boys and girls he illustrated Take a Number, O'Neill,
M. , Doubleday, 1968.

NAKATANI, Chiyoko

Native of Japan, she attended Japanese art schools and
later studied in Switzerland and France. In addition to
her own country, her work has been published in the
United States, England, and many European countries.
The artist has made her home in Tokyo. Her work in-
cludes the 1968 Children's Spring Book Festival Honor
Book (Picture Books) The Brave Little Goat of Monsieur
Séguin, Daudet, A. , adapted by, World, 1968.

NANKIVEL, Claudine

She grew up in Englewood, New Jersey. Claudine
Nankivel attended the Art Students League in New York
and also studied in France. For children she illustrated
Getting To Know Hong Kong, Joy, C. , Coward, 1962.

NEBEL, Gustave (Mimouca)

He was born in France. His work has been exhibited in
both America and Europe, and he has designed scenery
for the ballet in Paris. Many of his frescoes and murals
have been purchased by private collectors in America.
He wrote and illustrated Happy Old Engine, Funk, 1968.

NESS, Evaline (Michelow) 1911-

Illustrator-author, born in Union City, Ohio. Prior to
attending art school she studied library science and took
courses in education. She attended the Art Students
League in New York, the Art Institute in Chicago, and
the Accademia di Belle Arti in Rome. She has created
illustrations for magazines. In addition to living in
Rome, Evaline Ness has also visited Bangkok and traveled

throughout the Orient.   Several of her book illustrations
have been runners-up for the Caldecott Medal.   In 1967
she received the Caldecott Medal for her book Sam,
Bangs And Moonshine, Holt, 1966.   She also wrote and
illustrated: A Double Discovery, Scribner, 1965; Long,
Broad & Quickeye, Scribners, 1969; Mr. Miacca, Holt,
1967; Pavo And The Princess, Scribner, 1964.   (Authors
Of Books For Young People-rev. ed.)   ICB-3

NEWELL, Crosby see BONSALL, Crosby Barbara (Newell)

NICOLAS see MORDVINOFF, Nicolas

NINON see MACKNIGHT, Ninon

NISENSON, Samuel
   Designer and illustrator.   His drawings can be found in
   books about sports, nature, music, and biography.   Mr.
   Nisenson also created the "Minute Biographies" series.
   For young people he illustrated The Giant Book Of Sports,
   Davis, M. , Grosset, 1967.

OHLSSON, Ib   1935-
   He was born in Copenhagen where he attended the School
   of Decorative and Applied Arts.   He also studied at
   Randersgade Skole.   He spent two years in the Danish
   Civil Defense program and later traveled throughout
   Europe.   In addition to his work in advertising and graphic
   design, Ib Ohlsson has also illustrated textbooks.   The
   artist first came to America on a student grant in 1950
   and returned to live in Kew Gardens, New York in 1960.

Orbaan, Albert F. 1913-
His work for children includes: The Long and Dangerous
Journey, Craig, M., Norton, 1965; Philbert the Fearful,
Williams, J., Norton, 1966.   ICB-3

ORBAAN, Albert F. 1913-
He was born in Rome, Italy and came to the United
States at the age of eighteen. His father was an art
historian in the Netherlands. During World War II, he
served in Army Military Intelligence. Following the war,
he studied at the Art Students League. Before he became an artist, he was a reporter on a newspaper. His
home has been in New York City. His work includes:
No Room For A Dog, Holland, M., Random, 1959; The
Sound Of Axes, Smith, F., Rand, 1965.   ICB-2

OSBORN, Robert Chesley 1904-
He was born in Oshkosh, Wisconsin and later made his
home in Salisbury, Connecticut. He attended Yale University and the British Academy in Rome. He also
studied in Paris at the Académie Scandinav. Mr. Osborn
has written and illustrated books for adults in addition
to illustrating books for children. His drawings have
appeared in such magazines as Harper's and Life. For
boys and girls he illustrated: I Met A Man, Ciardi, J.,
Houghton, 1961; The Song Of Paul Bunyan & Tony Beaver,
Rees, E., Pantheon, 1964.   ICB-3

OXENBURY, Helen
She was born in Ipswich, Suffolk, England. After studying for two years at the Ipswich School of Art, she continued her art studies at London's Central School of Art.

She has been a theatrical designer in Israel and England
and once served as art director on a biblical film. Following her marriage to artist and writer John Burningham, she has been a free lance designer. Her book for
young people was Numbers of Things, Watts, 1968.

PAPIN, Joseph

He was born in St. Louis, Missouri and attended Ohio
State University in Columbus, Ohio. His work has
appeared in many magazines. He and his family have
lived in Matawan, New Jersey. Using artwork of seven-
teenth-century London as a basis, he illustrated Great
Fire of London, Weiss, D., Crown, 1968. He also illustrated Famous Pioneers, Folsom, F., Harvey House,
1963.

PARNALL, Peter 1936-

He was born in Syracuse, New York and grew up in
Connecticut and California. He received his education
at Cornell University and Pratt Institute School of Art.
Peter Parnall has been an art director for both a magazine and advertising firm. He and his family have
lived in New Milford, New Jersey. For young people
he illustrated A Tale of Middle Length, Shura, M.,
Atheneum, 1966.   ICB-3

PATON, Jane Elizabeth 1934-

She was born in London where she later studied at St.
Martin's School of Art and the Royal College of Art.
She has lived in Surrey and often visited with her parents
who moved to southern France. The artist once said

she used her sister's children as models for her draw-
ings. She illustrated the following books for young people:
Mr. Garden, Farjeon, E. , Walck, 1966; Ragged Robin,
Reeves, J. , Dutton, 1961.   ICB-3

PAUL, James see KOCSIS, James C.

PAYNE, Joan Balfour   1923-
She was born in Natchez, Mississippi and grew up in
Minneapolis, Minnesota where she received her education
and studied art.   Her first published work was in collab-
oration with her mother, writer Josephine Balfour Payne.
She married John Barber Dicks, Jr. , who has been a
professor of physics at the University of Tennessee Space
Institute in Sewanee.   For children she wrote and illus-
trated Pangur Ban, Hastings, 1966.   She also illustrated
Stable That Stayed, Payne, J. , Pellegrini & Cudahy, 1952.
                                             ICB-2, ICB-3

PAYSON, Dale   1943-
She was born in White Plains, New York and later lived
in Westport, Connecticut where she has worked with the
Young People's Division of the Famous Artists School.
She received her education at Endicott Junior College in
Beverly, Massachusetts and the School of Visual Arts in
New York.   The artist has also traveled abroad.   For
boys and girls she illustrated Ann Aurelia and Dorothy,
Carlson, N. , Harper, 1968.

PAYZANT, Charles
He has lived in Hollywood.   He achieved recognition as

92   Petersham, Maud (Fuller) 1890- Miska 1889-1960
the creator of a series of Christmas cards which depicted
America during the 1900's. Mr. Payzant has also been
known for his water colors. For young people he illustrated Little Wolf, Shannon, T., Whitman, 1954.

PETERSHAM, Maud (Fuller) 1890- Miska 1889-1960
Authors and illustrators, this husband and wife team have
contributed many books for children. Maud Petersham
was born in Kingston, New York, the daughter of a minister. A graduate of Vassar, she did further study at
the New York School of Fine and Applied Arts. Born
Petrezselyem Mihaly in Hungary, he changed his name
to Miska Petersham after his arrival in England. He
attended night classes in London in order to study art
and later came to New York where he continued his
painting. In 1946 the Petershams received the Caldecott
Medal for The Rooster Crows, Macmillan, 1945. They
also wrote: American ABC, Macmillan, 1941; Box With
Red Wheels, Macmillan, 1949; The Christ Child, Doubleday, 1931; Circus Baby, Macmillan, 1950. (Authors Of
Books For Young People-1964)   ICB-1, ICB-2, ICB-3

PETIE, Haris
She was born in Boulder Creek, California and attended
the Rochester Institute of Technology in New York. She
also studied art under Norman Rockwell in Paris. Her
illustrations have appeared in both magazines and books.
Mrs. Petie has made her home in Tenafly, New Jersey.
Her work includes: The Earth Around Us, Collins, H.,
adapted by, Dial Press, 1960; Getting to Know Colombia,
Halsell, G., Coward-McCann, 1964; Getting to Know

Pickard, Charles

Saudi Arabia, Phillips, T., Coward-McCann, 1963.

PICKARD, Charles

He was born in Yorkshire, England and studied at the
Harrogate School of Art and at London's Royal College
of Art. He received the Gold Medal of the Art Directors Club of Philadelphia in 1957. He has lived in London. His work includes: Mike's Gang, Weir, R., Abelard-Schuman, 1965; Worlds Lost and Found, Eisenberg,
A., Abelard-Schuman, 1964.

PINTO, Ralph

He was born in Brooklyn and attended New York City's
School of Visual Arts. The illustrator and his family
have resided in Hillsdale, New Jersey. His book illustrations include: The Magic Sack: A Lithuanian Folk-
tale, Rudolph, M., McGraw, 1967; Two Wise Children,
Graves, R., Harlin-Quist, 1966.

PIUSSI-CAMPBELL, Judy

She was born in South Bend, Indiana, the daughter of
writer M. Rudolph Campbell. After graduating from De
Pauw University in Greencastle, Indiana, she worked in
New York City as an illustrator and textile designer.
She married Pietro Piussi and lived in Florence, Italy
where her husband has been on the staff at the university.
Her book illustrations include: Poor Merlo, O'Neill, M.,
Atheneum, 1967; The Talking Crocodile, Campbell, M.,
adapted by, Atheneum, 1968.

PLUMMER, W. Kirtman

He attended Syracuse University, England's Brighton
School of Art, and graduated from the Philadelphia
College of Art. His illustrations have appeared in Good
Housekeeping and Holiday magazines. His work has been
exhibited in the New York City and Philadelphia Art Di-
rectors' shows. For young people he illustrated Picture
Map Geography of Western Europe, Wohlrabe, R., Lip-
pincott, 1967.

POLITI, Leo 1908-

Author-illustrator, born in Fresno, California. When he
was seven, his family moved to Italy. At the age of
fifteen, he was awarded a scholarship for the Institute
of Monza near Milan. Mr. Politi returned to the United
States and has lived in Los Angeles. In 1950 he re-
ceived the Caldecott Medal for his picture book, Song Of
The Swallows, Junior Literary Guild and Scribner, 1949.
Other titles include: Boat For Peppe, Scribner, 1950;
The Butterflies Come, Scribner, 1957; Juanita, Scribner,
1948; Little Leo, Junior Literary Guild and Scribner,
1951; Mieko, Golden Gate, 1969; The Mission Bell,
Scribner, 1953; Moy Moy, Scribner, 1960; Saint Francis
And The Animals, Scribner, 1959. (Authors Of Books
For Young People-1964)   ICB-1, ICB-2, ICB-3

POLSENO, Jo

He received a degree in Fine Arts from New Haven's
Whitney Art School, and he also studied at the Ecole des
Beaux Arts in Marseilles. In addition to books, his work
has appeared in many magazines. Mr. Polseno has en-

joyed sports and has been a pro football fan. His work
includes: Cop's Kid, Corbett, S. , Little, 1968; Fine
Eggs and Fancy Chickens, Marks, M. , Holt, 1956;
When My Father Was a Little Boy, Lonergan, J. , Watts,
1961.

PORTER, George

Illustrator and painter, born in Perry, Florida. He
attended the Brooklyn Museum School and Phoenix Art
School in New York, and the Ringling School of Art in
Sarasota, Florida. His home has been in Katonah, New
York. Goerge Porter has painted portraits in addition
to illustrating magazines and books for children. His
book illustrations include The Christmas Tree Mystery
(A Junior Literary Guild Selection), St. John, W. , Viking, 1969.

PORTER, Jean Macdonald 1906-

She was born in Ardmore, Pennsylvania, grew up there
and in New Jersey, and studied at the Philadelphia
Museum School of Industrial Art. Her ancestry has in-
cluded a painter, sculptor, and singer. Her husband
Pliny Porter was among many who encouraged her to
draw and paint. Mrs. Porter made numerous charcoal
sketches of service men and women in hospitals during
World War II. She has also made many sketches of the
Soap Box Derby in White Plains, New York. For boys
and girls she illustrated: Quacko And The Elps (A Junior
Literary Guild selection), Froman, R. , McKay, 1964;
A Race For Bill, Wallace, M. , Nelson, 1951.   ICB-2

POWERS, Richard M.   1921-

His pseudonym is Terry Gorman. He grew up in Chicago
where he was born. He later made his home in Ridge-
field, Connecticut but has also lived in Maine, New York,
and Vermont. The artist attended Loyola University and
the Chicago Art Institute. He also studied at the University of Illinois Art School in Urbana and the New School
for Social Research in New York. In addition to his
work in book illustration, Richard Powers has written
both children's and adult books. He has also been a
painter. He served in the Army during World War II.
For young readers he illustrated: David And Goliath,
DeRegniers, B. , Viking, 1965; Musical Instruments Of
Africa, Dietz, B. , Day, 1965.   ICB-2, ICB-3

PRICE, Garrett 1896-

Cartoonist and artist. He was born in Bucyrus, Kansas,
grew up in Saratoga, Wyoming, and attended the University of Wyoming in Laramie. He also studied at the Art
Institute in Chicago and in New York and Paris. His
home has been in Westport, Connecticut. Garrett Price
served as editorial and sports cartoonist on the Great
Lakes Navy Bulletin during World War I. He has illustrated many magazine covers and has been on the New
Yorker staff since 1925. For children he illustrated
The Honey Boat (A Junior Literary Guild selection),
Burroughs, P. , Little, 1968.   ICB-3

PURSELL, Weimer

Free-lance illustrator and designer. He attended the
Chicago Art Institute and also studied at the New Bauhaus

School of Design.   Prior to devoting all of his time to
art, Mr. Pursell had been a college instructor.   For
young people he illustrated Biography of An Atom, Bron-
owski, J., Harper, 1965.

PYLE, Howard   1853-1911
Artist, painter, teacher.   Born in Wilmington, Delaware,
he attended the Art Students League in New York.   He
died at the age of fifty-eight in Florence, Italy.   His
drawings have appeared in books by other writers in addition to his illustrations for children.   His work has
also appeared in Harper's Monthly.   For boys and girls
he wrote and illustrated: Men Of Iron, Harper, 1904;
Otto Of The Silver Hand, Scribner, 1920.

QUACKENBUSH, Robert Mead 1929-
Born in California, he grew up in Phoenix, Arizona,
and graduated from the Art Center School in Los Angeles.
Following military service he studied at the New School
for Social Research in New York City.   In addition to
book illustration, Robert Quackenbush has illustrated for
magazines.   His work first appeared in Sports Illustrated
in 1962.   He has traveled abroad on magazine assignments and has made his home in New York City.   His
favorite media of art has been woodcuts.   For young
people he illustrated: Horatio, Clymer, E., Atheneum,
1968; I Feel the Same Way, Moore, L., Atheneum, 1967;
Two Worlds of Damyan, Bloch, M., Atheneum, 1966.

ICB-3

RAIBLE, Alton Robert   1918-

He was born in Modesto, California and studied at the
California College of Arts and Crafts in Oakland.   He has
worked in a bank and a shipyard.   Mr. Raible later
taught art at the College of Marin in Kentfield, California.
His home has been in San Anselmo, California.   His
work includes: Season of Ponies, Snyder, Z. , Atheneum,
1964; The Velvet Room (A Junior Literary Guild selection), Snyder, Z. , Atheneum, 1965.   ICB-3

RASKIN, Ellen   1928-

She was born in Milwaukee and studied at the University
of Wisconsin.   Her work has appeared in magazines and
on book jackets and has received much recognition.   In
1966 her book Nothing Ever Happens On My Block (Atheneum, 1966) was designated a Prize Book by the Herald Tribune in the Spring Children's Book Festival.   Her
home has been in New York City.   Her work includes:
A Book To Begin On Books, Bartlett, S. , Hold, 1968;
The King Of Men, Coolidge, O. , Houghton, 1966. ICB-3

RAYNES, John

Artist and writer, born in Australia.   He grew up in
England where he attended the Royal College of Art in
London.   Mr. Raynes has worked in advertising and has
written books in addition to his career as an illustrator.
His work has also appeared in magazines.   For young
people he illustrated What Car Is That?, Lent, H. ,
Dutton, 1969.

REED, Veronica see SHERMAN, Theresa

REID, Bill

The descendant of a Haida Indian chief (Charlie Glad-
stone), he has done a great deal of research on Haida
art. He has also created jewelry which has reflected
this art form. For boys and girls he illustrated Raven's
Cry, Harris, C., Atheneum, 1966.

RÉTHI, Lili 1894-

Artist-illustrator, born in Austria. She became an
American citizen after coming to the United States in
1939. In addition to book illustration, the artist has had
her work exhibited in many museums. New York University had a permanent exhibit of Miss Réthi's work at the
Wallace Clark Center. For young people she has illustrated: The First Book of Ancient Egypt, Robinson, C.,
Watts, 1961; First Book of Medieval Man, Sobol, D.,
Watts, 1959.

RIBBONS, Ian 1924-

He was born in London and studied at the Beckenham
School of Art in Kent and at London's Royal College of
Art. He served in the Army in India and Burma. Mr.
Ribbons has been an art instructor in the Colleges of
Guildford and Brighton and at the Hornsey College of
Art in London. His interests have included music and
travel. He wrote Monday 21, October 1805, David White,
1968 and illustrated Linnets and Valerians, Goudge, E.,
Coward-McCann, 1964.   ICB-2, ICB-3

RICE, Elizabeth

Her illustrations have appeared in the books written by

Adda Mai Sharp. She has been known to be interested in
all new aspects in the field of art, and this interest has
been reflected in her work. She illustrated Secret Places,
Sharp, A., Steck, 1955.

RINGI, Kjell

Swedish born artist and author, Kjell Ringi came to the
United States as a student. In 1967 he received recog-
nition as an artist on a visit to New York. His work has
included books, magazine illustrations, and paintings.
For young people he wrote and illustrated The Stranger
(A Junior Literary Guild selection), Random, 1968.

RISWOLD, Gilbert

He was born in Chicago, Illinois and grew up in Oak
Park, Illinois and Salt Lake City, Utah. He has worked
in the motion picture industry and on Air Corps Training
Films. His work has received several awards which
include: an award from the Art Directors Club of Chicago
and in 1964 an Award for Excellence from the Society of
Illustrators in New York. The Riswolds have lived in
Newtown, Connecticut. His work includes: Happy Prince,
Wilde, O., Duckworth, 1952; Round Robin (rev. ed.),
Davis, L., Scribner, 1962; School Bell In the Valley,
Carlson, N., Harcourt, 1963.   ICB-3

RIVOLI, Mario 1943-

Artist and designer, born in New York City. He studied
in New York at the Art Students League, School of Industrial Arts, and the School of Visual Arts. At one time
Mario Rivoli worked in fashion illustration and fabric de-

sign. He was the recipient of the 1965 Society of Illustrators Award. The artist has lived and operated a shop
called "The Tunnel of Love" in New York City. His
work includes: Do Tigers Ever Bite Kings? (A Junior
Literary Guild selection), Wersba, B. , Atheneum, 1966;
A Song For Clowns (A Junior Literary Guild selection),
Wersba, B. , Atheneum, 1965.   ICB-3

ROCKWELL, Norman 1894-
Born in New York City, he studied at the National Academy of Design, Chase Art School, and the Art Students
League. When he was seventeen, he had received assignments to illustrate several publications. He once served
as Art Editor for Boys' Life. His cover drawings often
appeared on the Saturday Evening Post, and he also painted for the Boy Scout calendar for many years. He has
lived in Arlington, Vermont. For boys and girls he
illustrated: The Adventures Of Huckleberry Finn,
Clemens, S. , Hermitage Press, 1940; Dead End School,
Coles, R. , Little, 1968.   ICB-1

ROGERS, Carol
Artist and designer, born in Waco, Texas. Her home
has been near Austin. She received her B. A. degree
in design from Texas Woman's University at Denton.
Carol Rogers has worked in advertising and illustrated
textbooks in addition to picture books for children. She
has enjoyed animals and raising flowers as hobbies. For
young readers she illustrated: A Good Morning's Work
(A Junior Literary Guild selection), Zimelman, N. ,
Steck, 1968; Once When I Was Five, Zimelman, N. ,

Steck, 1967.

ROJANKOVSKY, Feodor 1891-
Illustrator, author, born in Mitava, Russia. He attended
the Academy of Art in Moscow. In World War I he was
an officer in the Russian Army. Feodor Rojankovsky has
been art director of the Opera in Pazan, Poland and also
in a Polish publishing house. He came to the United
States in 1941. In 1956 he won the Caldecott Medal for
Frog Went A-Courtin' (retold by John Langstaff), Harcourt,
1955. Juvenile books include: Animals In The Zoo,
Knopf, 1962; Animals On The Farm, Knopf, 1967; A
Crowd Of Cows, Graham, J., Harcourt, 1968; Daniel
Boone, Averill, E., Harper, 1945. (Authors Of Books
For Young People-1964)   ICB-1, ICB-2, ICB-3

ROSE, Gerald 1935-
He was born in Hong Kong and studied at the Royal
Academy in London. His wife, a schoolteacher and
author, encouraged him to illustrate children's books. In
1960 he was awarded England's Kate Greenaway Medal.
Mr. Rose has taught in the Graphic Design School of the
Maidstone College of Art. He and his wife have lived
in Kent, England. His work includes: The Big River,
Rose, E., Norton, 1962; Dan McDougall and the Bulldozer,
Pender, L., Abelard-Schuman, 1963; The Story of the
Pied Piper, Ireson, B., Barnes, 1961.   ICB-3

ROSS, John 1921-
Artist, lecturer, teacher, born in New York City. He
and his artist-wife Clare Romano Ross have lived in

Englewood, New Jersey. Mr. Ross attended New York's
Cooper Union School of Art and also studied in France
and Italy. Both Mr. and Mrs. Ross have lectured and
lived abroad and have received many art awards. Both
have also been on the staffs of Pratt Institute in Brooklyn
and the New School for Social Research in New York.
Mr. Ross has been a past President of the Society of
American Graphic Artists. For young people he illustrated Sprints And Distances, Morrison, L. (comp.),
Crowell, 1965.   ICB-3

SADER, Lillian

Artist-designer. After graduating from the Chicago Art
Institute, she continued her studies at the University of
California at Berkeley. Exhibitions of her work have
been held at Art Director's shows in San Francisco and
Chicago and in museums and galleries. Lillian Sader
has been associated with one of the leading design studios
in this country. Her home has been in Berkeley, Calif-
ornia. For children she illustrated The King Who Rides
A Tiger and Other Folk Tales From Nepal, Hitchcock,
P., Parnassus, 1967.

SANDBERG, Lasse E. M.   1924-

He was born in Stockholm, Sweden and studied at Anders
Beckman's Art School. He has been a cartoonist and
photographer in addition to illustrating books for boys and
girls. He has won several awards including the 1965
Elsa Beskow Plaque (Swedish Librarians' prize for best
children's book illustrations). The Sandbergs have lived
in Karlstad, Sweden. He and his wife Inger collaborated
on What Anna Saw, Lothrop, 1964.   ICB-3

SANDIN, Joan

   Born in Watertown, Wisconsin, she spent her childhood
   in the southwestern part of the United States. She graduated from the University of Arizona at Tucson. Prior
   to making her home in New York City, she traveled in
   Europe. As a member of the New York Council of
   American Youth Hostels, she has enjoyed taking young
   people on camping and cycling trips. She illustrated
   "Hey, What's Wrong With This One?", Wojciechowska,
   M. , Harper, 1969.

SAPIEHA, Christine

   Born in Poland, she came to the United States in 1939.
   She studied at Georgetown University and the Parsons
   School of Design. Miss Sapieha has been Assistant Art
   Director of The Reporter and once did illustrations for
   the British School of Archaeology in Greece. She has
   also worked for the Metropolitan Museum of Art in New
   York City. She illustrated Hermit Crab Lives In A
   Shell, Stephens, W. , Holiday, 1969.

SAVAGE, Steele 1900-

   He was born in Detroit, Michigan and later made his
   home in New York City. He studied at the Detroit School
   of Fine Arts, Chicago Art Institute, and the Slade School
   of Fine Art in London. In addition to book illustration,
   Mr. Savage has been a magazine illustrator, set and
   costume designer, and advertising artist. He once lived
   and painted in the West Indies. For children he illustrated: Andrew Carnegie, Judson, C. , Follett, 1964;
   Bible Dictionary For Boys and Girls, Komroff, M. ,

Winston, 1957; Patch, A Baby Mink, Voight, V., Putnam,
1965.   ICB-2

SCHACHNER, Erwin

He was born in Austria and came to the United States
in 1940. A graduate of the Philadelphia Museum School,
he also studied at Pratt Institute in Brooklyn, New York.
He has worked in advertising, printing, and illustrated
for magazines. His wood and linoleum cuts have been
exhibited in New York and Philadelphia. Mr. Schachner
has lived in New York City. He created the wood engravings for The Story of Lighthouses, Chase, M., Norton, 1965.

SCHINDELMAN, Joseph 1923-

He was born in New York, studied at the Art Students
League, WPA art classes, and New York City College.
He has worked in radio and has been an art director in
an advertising agency. A book which he illustrated was
selected as one of ten best-illustrated books of 1963 by
the New York Times. His work includes: Charlie and
the Chocolate Factory, Dahl, R., Knopf, 1964; The Mar-
velous March of Jean François, Raymond, J., Doubleday, 1965; Voices in the Meadow (A Junior Literary
Guild selection), Bosworth, J., Doubleday, 1964. ICB-3

SCHOENHERR, John Carl 1935-

He was born in New York City, studied at Pratt Institute
and the Art Students League, and later lived on a farm
in Stockton, New Jersey. In addition to book illustration
for both children and adults, he has illustrated science

fiction magazines and paperback book covers.   Mr.
Schoenherr has belonged to the National Speleological
Society, the New York Zoological Society, and the Society
of Illustrators.   He was winner of first prize at the Na-
tional Speleological Society Salon in 1963 and was the
recipient of the World Science Fiction Award in 1965.
The artist has also been honored by the Society of Illus-
trators.   For children he illustrated Mississippi Possum,
Miles, M., Little, 1965.   He also wrote and illustrated
Barn, Little, 1968.   ICB-3

SCHONGUT, Emanuel
Artist-teacher.   After graduating from Pratt Institute,
he did further study at the Pratt Graphic Art Center and
Art Students League.   Mr. Schongut has been an art instructor at Pratt and has also designed and illustrated
book jackets.   His work has appeared in such magazines
as Ingenue and Harper's.   For children he illustrated
Tomorrow's Children: 18 Tales of Fantasy and Science
Fiction, Asimov, I., Doubleday, 1967.

SCHREIBER, Georges 1904-
Born in Brussels, Belgium, he studied in Germany at
Kunstgewerbeschule, Elberfield and at the Academy of
Fine Arts in Berlin and Duesseldorf.   He came to the
United States at the age of twenty-four and ten years
later became a naturalized citizen.   His illustrations have
appeared in many magazines, and he has designed posters
for the U.S. Treasury Department.   Mr. Schreiber's
work has been included in the permanent collections of
many museums and colleges.   He married Lillian Yamin,

and they have lived in New York City. His work includes:
Pancakes---Paris, Bishop, C., Viking, 1947; Ride On
The Wind, Dalgliesh, A. (told by), Scribner, 1956.

ICB-2

SCHUYLER, Remington 1884-1955

Born in Buffalo, New York, he attended Washington University in St. Louis, the Art Students League in New York,
and also studied abroad. His father was a critic on the
St. Louis Post Dispatch, and his mother was an artist
and musician. He was active in Boy Scouts and wrote
several of their Merit Badge pamphlets. He taught art
and was Artist in Residence at Missouri Valley College
in Marshall, Missouri. He illustrated Great White
Buffalo, McCracken, H., Lippincott, 1946. ICB-1, ICB-2

SEGAWA, Yasuo 1932-

He was born in Okazaki City, Japan. He received first
prize in the Japan Tourist Poster Contest in 1959 and
1960. In Tokyo he has painted and worked in sculpture
using both European and Japanese techniques. For young
people he illustrated The Many Lives of Chio and Goro,
Lifton, B., Norton, 1968.

SEITZ, Patricia

Artist-teacher. She graduated from the Maryland Institute
of Art in Baltimore where she also taught an art class
for children. She and her husband, also an artist, have
lived in Minneapolis, Minnesota. She illustrated Ride
On! Ride On! An Easter Season Story for Children,
Martin, S., Augsburg Publishing House, 1968.

SELIG, Sylvie

Born in France, she studied at the École des Beaux
Arts in Paris. Her work has received recognition in
France and also won the 1968 Graphic Prize for Children
at the International Children's Book Fair in Bologna,
Italy. She and her husband have made their home in
Paris. She illustrated Etienne-Henri And Gri-Gri, Sur-
any, A., Holiday, 1969.

SENDAK, Maurice 1928-

Author-illustrator, born in Brooklyn, New York. He
attended the Art Students League. During high school
he illustrated his first book. Meindert DeJong's The
Wheel On The School (Harper, 1954) with pictures by
Maurice Sendak won the Newbery Medal in 1955. Other
juvenile books include: Nutshell Library, Harper, 1962;
The Sign On Rosie's Door, Harper, 1960; Very Far
Away, Harper, 1957; Where The Wild Things Are (winner of the 1964 Caldecott Medal), Harper, 1963. (Authors Of Books For Young People-1964)   ICB-2   ICB-3

SHAW, Charles

A native of Texas, he has made his home in Austin.
His work has been exhibited in art director's shows in
Texas and Colorado. In addition to book illustration,
Mr. Shaw has worked in advertising firms. For child-
ren he illustrated House Upon A Rock (A Junior Literary
Guild selection), Pedersen, E., Atheneum, 1968.

SHENTON, Edward 1895-

Artist and teacher, born in Pottstown, Pennsylvania.

Shepard, Ernest Howard 1879-

He attended the Philadelphia Museum School of Industrial
Art and the Pennsylvania Academy of the Fine Arts. He
also studied in Paris. He married writer Barbara Webster and has illustrated her books. Their home has been
in West Chester, Pennsylvania. Mr. Shenton has been
associated with Philadelphia's Moore College of Art as
head of its Department of Illustration. In addition to
teaching and illustrating, he has also written books and
stories for magazines. For children he illustrated Find-
ing Out About The Incas, Burland, C., Lothrop, 1962.
He also wrote and illustrated On Wings For Freedom,
Macrae Smith, 1942. ICB-1, ICB-2

SHEPARD, Ernest Howard 1879-

He was born in London and studied at Heatherley School
of Art and the Royal Academy Schools. In his early
twenties he exhibited his first picture at the Royal
Academy. During World War I, he served in the Royal
Artillery. He was on the staff of Punch and gained fame
as a children's book illustrator when he illustrated the
books written by A. A. Milne. Mr. Shepard has lived
in Lodsworth, Sussex. His work includes: When We
Were Very Young, Milne, A., Dutton, 1924; The Wind
In The Willows, Grahame, K., Scribner's, 1908.

ICB-1, ICB-2

SHEPARD, Mary Eleanor 1909-

She was born on Christmas Day in England, the daughter
of distinguished illustrator E. H. Shepard. She studied
in Paris and at the Slade School of Fine Art and the
Central School of Art in London. She married a former

editor of Punch named E. V. Knox, and they have lived
in London. Her work has received several awards, and
she has had exhibitions in London galleries. She illustrated Mary Poppins From A to Z, Travers, P. , Harcourt, 1962.   ICB-2, ICB-3

SHERMAN, Theresa 1916-
Her pseudonym is Veronica Reed. She married David
Rosenberg and has lived in Manhattan where she was
born. Her childhood was spent in Brooklyn, and she has
lived in France. In addition to private study, Theresa
Sherman attended both the American Artists School and
Art Students League in New York. She has exhibited her
work in galleries, conducted painting and ceramic classes
for adults, and taught painting, puppetry, and sculpture
to children. She illustrated: Big Puppy And Little Puppy,
Black, I. , Holiday, 1960; Muggsy, Holland, M. , Knopf,
1959.   ICB-2

SHIMIN, Symeon 1902-
He was born in Astrakhan, Russia and came to the United
States at the age of ten. He studied at Cooper Union and
painted in George Luk's studio; however, most of his art
training came from studying paintings in the museums of
Spain and France. He has painted murals in the Depart-
ment of Justice building in Washington, D. C. and the
United States Post Office building in Tonawanda, New
York. He held his first one-man exhibition in 1961. The
artist married a sculptor and has lived in New York City.
His work includes: All Except Sammy (A Junior Literary
Guild selection), Cretan, G. , Little, 1966; One Small

Shore, Robert 1924-

Blue Bead, Schweitzer, B., Macmillan, 1965; Outdoor
Wonderland, Wilson, R., Lothrop, 1961.   ICB-2, ICB-3

SHORE, Robert 1924-
Painter, sculptor, born in New York City. He studied
at the Cranbrook Academy of Art in Michigan and at the
Art Students League in New York. In 1952 he was award-
ed a Fulbright Fellowship and in 1966 received the Gold
Medal from the Society of Illustrators. He has taught
at the School of Visual Arts. For children he illustrated
The Big Pile Of Dirt, Clymer, E., Holt, 1968.   ICB-3

SHORTALL, Leonard
He was born in Seattle, Washington, attended the University of Washington, and later made his home in Westport,
Connecticut. His illustrations have appeared in such national magazines as Farm Journal and Woman's Day. He
has also written and illustrated his own books and worked
in advertising. His drawings can be found in Pecos Bill
And The Mustang, Felton, H., Prentice-Hall, 1965.
ICB-2, ICB-3

SHULEVITZ, Uri 1935-
Artist and author, born in Warsaw, Poland. He grew
up in Poland, France, and Israel where he studied at
the Tel Aviv Academy of Art. After coming to the
United States in 1959, he continued his studies at the
Museum of Art in Brooklyn, New York. His work has
received recognition from the American Institute of
Graphic Arts and the Society of Illustrators. He married
an artist and has lived in New York City. He was

awarded the 1969 Caldecott Medal for The Fool Of The
World And The Flying Ship, Ransome, A., Farrar, 1968.
He wrote and illustrated The Moon In My Room, Harper,
1963. Other juvenile books he illustrated include: The
Carpet Of Solomon, Ish-Kishor, S., Pantheon, 1966;
Maximilian's World, Stolz, M., Harper, 1966. (Authors
Of Books For Young People-rev. ed.)   ICB-3

SIBAL, Joseph
Born in Vienna, he came to the United States when he was
quite young. Mr. Sibal studied at the Art Students League,
the National Academy of Design, and the Polytechnic Institute in Brooklyn. Prior to painting birds, he was an
industrial artist. He has visited zoos throughout the
United States and Europe, and in 1952 his paintings of
birds were exhibited in New York City libraries. They
were later published in Life magazine. For young people
he illustrated Giant Birds and Monsters Of The Air (A
Junior Literary Guild selection), Wise, W., Putnam,
1969.

SIBERELL, Anne
She was born in California and attended UCLA and the
Chouinard Art Institute in Los Angeles. Mrs. Peter
Siberell and her family have lived in New Canaan, Connecticut. In addition to her work as an illustrator, she
has been both a print maker and painter. She has also
worked for an architectural firm. For children she illustrated: A Donkey For a King, Beatty, J., Macmillan,
1966; Rainbow Over All, Eastwick, I., McKay, 1967.

SIBLEY, Don 1922-

He was born in Hornell, New York and later made his
home in Roxbury, Connecticut. He completed his education at Pratt Institute in Brooklyn after serving as
a pilot in World War II. His career has included advertising and promotion work in addition to children's
book illustrations. These include: Skinny, Burch, R.,
Viking, 1964; Tyler, Wilkin, And Skee, Burch, R.,
Viking 1963.   ICB-3

SIDJAKOV, Nicolas 1924-

He was born in Riga, Latvia. He attended the École des
Beaux Arts in Paris in order to study painting. He has
been a free-lance designer and illustrator. He married
an American girl in Paris, but they have lived in the
United States since 1954. He has had a studio in San
Francisco. His first illustrations in a children's book
appeared in Laura N. Baker's adaptation of an old English Christmas carol The Friendly Beasts, Parnassus,
1957. He also illustrated two books written by Ruth
Robbins: Baboushka And The Three Kings (winner of the
1961 Caldecott Medal), Parnassus, 1960; The Emperor
And Drummer Boy, Parnassus, 1962. (Authors Of Books
For Young People-1964)   ICB-1, ICB-2, ICB-3

SILVERMAN, Burton Philip 1928-

Illustrator, painter, born in Brooklyn, New York. Burt
Silverman studied at the Art Students League and at
Columbia University in New York. He has worked in a
studio apartment overlooking the Hudson River in New
York City. For young people he illustrated The Adven-

tures Of Tom Leigh (A Junior Literary Guild selection),
Bentley, P., Doubleday, 1966.   ICB-3

SILVERMAN, Melvin Frank 1931-1966
Illustrator, painter, teacher. Born in Denver, Colorado,
Mel Silverman studied and graduated from the Chicago Art
Institute. Prior to his death at the age of thirty-five, he
worked as a display designer in New York City. He also
taught graphics in Israel at Ein Harod. His paintings can
be found in permanent collections in museums and univer-
sities. For children he illustrated My First Geography
Of The Panama Canal, Sondergaard, A., Little, 1960.
He also wrote and illustrated Hymie's Fiddle, World, 1960.
                                                    ICB-3

SIMONT, Marc 1915-
Illustrator-author, born in Paris. He studied in Paris at
the André Lhote School, Académie Julien, and the Académie Ranson. He also studied in New York at the National Academy of Design. Marc Simont's work has included magazine illustrations, portraits, and visual aids
for the Army. Mr. Simont and his family have lived in
West Cornwall, Connecticut and in New York City. In
1957 he received the Caldecott Medal for his illustrations
in A Tree Is Nice (written by Janice May Udry), Harper,
1956. He also illustrated The Earth Is Your Spaceship,
Schwartz, J., McGraw, 1963. (Authors Of Books For
Young People-1964)   ICB-2, ICB-3

SLOBODKIN, Louis 1903-
Sculptor, illustrator, author. He grew up in Albany,

Smith, Alvin 1933-

New York and studied at the Beaux Arts Institute of Design in New York. He has illustrated children's books
for various authors, including James Thurber's Many
Moons (Harcourt, 1943), the winner of the 1944 Caldecott
Medal.   Mr. Slobodkin married Florence Gersh.   Juvenile
contributions include: Adventures Of Arab, Macmillan,
1946; Amiable Giant, Macmillan, 1955; Circus, April
1st, Macmillan, 1953; Dinny And Danny, Macmillan, 1951;
Excuse Me! Certainly!, Vanguard, 1959; Hustle And
Bustle, Macmillan, 1948; Space Ship Under The Apple
Tree, Macmillan, 1952.   (Authors Of Books For Young
People-1964)   ICB-1, ICB-2, ICB-3

SMITH, Alvin 1933-

He was born in Gary, Indiana and graduated from the
State University of Iowa.   He received his master's degree from the University of Illinois and did additional
work at Teachers College, Columbia University.   Atlanta
University Permanent Collection of Contemporary American Art and the Dayton Art Institute had his paintings in
their collections.   He has taught art in Kansas City,
Kansas, Dayton, Ohio and at Queens College of the City
of New York University.   He and his wife Pauline, a
teacher, have lived in New York City.   In addition to
illustrating the 1965 Newbery Award winner Shadow Of
A Bull, Wojciechowska, M., Atheneum, 1964, he also
illustrated The Nitty Gritty, Bonham, F., Dutton, 1968.
                                              ICB-3

SMITH, Lawrence Beall 1909-

Born in Washington, D. C., he grew up in Indiana and

Illinois. He received his education in Chicago at the Art
Institute and the University of Chicago. He married an
artist and has lived in Cross River, New York. The
artist served as an artist war correspondent during World
War II. For boys and girls he illustrated: Girls Are
Silly, Nash, O., Watts, 1962; Toby And The Nighttime,
Horgan, P., Ariel, 1963.   ICB-3

SNYDER, Jerome 1916-
Art director and illustrator, born in New York City. He
married an artist, and they have lived in Brooklyn. He
has done magazine illustrations and worked in advertising.
Jerome Snyder has been an Art Director for Scientific
American magazine and prior to this was Art Director
for Sports Illustrated. The artist has been the recipient
of many awards from New York's Art Directors Club and
the Society of Illustrators. For young people he illustrated: One Day In Elizabethan England, Kirtland, G., Harcourt, 1962; Umbrellas, Hats, and Wheels, Rand, A.,
Harcourt, 1961; Scientists and Scoundrels, Silverberg, R.,
Crowell, 1965.   ICB-3

SOLBERT, Ronni G. 1925-
She was born in Washington, D. C., grew up in Chicago
and Rochester, New York, and later graduated from
Vassar. She studied at the Cranbrook Academy of Art
and received a Fulbright Fellowship to India. She has
taught art to children and worked for the International
Red Cross Conference in Stockholm. In 1959 she had a
one-woman show at the Museum of Modern Art. Her
home has been in New York City. Books which she illus-

Sorel, Edward 1929-
trated for young people include: The Pushcart War, Merrill, J., Scott, 1964; The Superlative Horse (A Junior
Literary Guild selection), Merrill, J., Scott, 1961; Woody
and Me, Neville, M., Pantheon Bks., 1966.

ICB-2, ICB-3

SOREL, Edward 1929-
He was born in New York City where he later studied at
Cooper Union. He has done caricature and political sat-
ire, and his work has appeared in the Realist and Ram-
parts. One of the founders of Push Pin Studios, he has
also been a staff artist for Esquire and CBS. He has
received awards from the American Institute of Graphic
Arts and the Art Directors Club of New York. He mar-
ried Nancy Caldwell, and they have lived in Carmel, New
York. His work includes: The Duck In The Gun (A Junior
Literary Guild selection), Cowley, J., Doubleday, 1969;
Gwendolyn The Miracle Hen, Sherman, N., Golden, 1961;
King Carlo Of Capri, Miller, W., Harcourt, 1958.

ICB-3

SPIER, Peter 1927-
He was born in Amsterdam, Holland where he attended
Rijksakademie Voor Beeldende Kunsten. He served in the
Royal Netherlands Navy and later was Junior Editor of
Elsevier's Weekly in Holland. In 1951 he came to Hous-
ton, Texas where Elsevier's had a branch office. His
book The Fox Went Out On A Chilly Night (Doubleday,
1961) was runner-up for the Caldecott Medal in 1962. Mr.
Spier became an American citizen and has lived in Port
Washington, Long Island, New York. He illustrated:

Standon, Edward Cyril 1929-

Island City (A Junior Literary Guild selection), Davis,
L., Doubleday, 1961; London Bridge Is Falling Down!,
Doubleday, 1967; To Market! To Market!, Doubleday,
1967. ICB-2, ICB-3

STANDON, Edward Cyril 1929-
Artist and cartoonist. He grew up in London where he
was born and later attended St. Martin's School of Art.
He has been a musician and worked in animation, in addition to his work as a book illustrator. He has illustrated many of his wife's stories which includes The Tin
Can Tortoise, Standon, A., Coward, 1965. ICB-3

STEIG, William 1907-
New Yorker cartoonist, author, born in New York City.
Mr. Steig's family were artists, and so were his children: Lucy, a painter, and Jeremy who has also been a
jazz flautist. The Steigs have lived in Greenwich Village. Roland the Minstrel Pig, Windmill, 1968, was his
first book for children. He also created: CDB!, Simon
and Schuster, 1968 and Sylvester and the Magic Pebble,
Windmill, 1969 (1970 Caldecott Medal winner).

STEIN, Harve 1904-
Born in Chicago, Illinois where he later studied at the
Art Institute. He also attended the Académie Julian in
Paris and the Art Students League in New York. Mr.
Stein has been head of the Illustrations Department of the
Rhode Island School of Design. His home has been in
Noank, Connecticut. He illustrated Benjamin Franklin:
First Great American, Tottle, J., Houghton, 1958.
ICB-2

STEINBERG, David Michael

Artist, teacher, musician. He attended Harvard and
Columbia Universities, and the Université de Paris.
Some of his illustrations have been done in collaboration
with his father, Isador Steinberg. Chemistry and astron-
omy have been his hobbies, and he has worked in research laboratories in biochemistry. In addition to his
art work, David Steinberg has taught French literature
and has written songs. He has belonged to Phi Beta
Kappa and Mensa. For children he illustrated Bionics,
Halacy, D., Holiday, 1965.

STEVENS: Mary E. 1920-1966

She was born and grew up in Bar Harbor, Maine. She
received her education at Boston's Vesper George School
of Art and the Art Students League in New York. In addition to illustrating books for children, Miss Stevens also illustrated stories for Story Parade and Child Life
magazines. Puppetry, sports, and the theatre were her
special interests. Mary Stevens died in 1966 at the age
of forty-six. Juvenile books which she illustrated include: Have You Seen My Brother?, Guilfoile, E., Follett, 1962; The Real Hole, Cleary, B., Morrow, 1960;
Two Dog Biscuits, Cleary, B., Morrow, 1961.

                                        ICB-2   ICB-3

STEWART, Arvis L.

Born in Texas, he later made his home in New York
City. He attended the Texas Technological College in
Lubbock where he studied art and design. The artist
has enjoyed carpentry, fishing, and nature as special

interests in addition to printmaking and the fine arts.
He illustrated The New Friend, Zolotow, C., Abelard,
1968.

STIRNWEIS, Shannon

He was born in Portland, Oregon and studied at the Los
Angeles Art Center School. He once served abroad with
the United States Army as an illustrator of instructional
materials. Mr. Stirnweis has made his home in New
York City. His work includes: Book To Begin On Numbers, Waller, L., Holt, 1960; Getting To Know Tangan-
yika, Joy, C., Coward-McCann, 1962; Getting To Know
The British West Indies, Gudmundson, S., Coward-Mc-
Cann, 1962.

STOBBS, William 1914-

He was born in South Shields, England and has lived in
Richmond, Surrey, England. He studied at King Edward
VI School of Art and received both a B.A. and M.A.
degree in the History of Art from Durham University.
Prior to being Principal of Maidstone College of Art, Mr.
Stobbs was associated with the London School of Printing
and Graphic Arts as Head of the Design Department. He
has belonged to the Society of Industrial Artists. He il-
lustrated: Kashtanka, Chekhov, A., Walck, 1961; Walter
Raleigh, Syme, R., Morrow, 1962.   ICB-2, ICB-3

STONE, Helen 1904-

Born in Englewood, New Jersey, she attended the Art
Students League and the New York School of Fine and
Applied Art. She also studied in Paris. She has been

Stover, Jo Ann
121

a teacher and worked in the field of commercial art in addition to illustrating books for young people. Mrs. Stone has traveled in Europe and the West Indies and has made her home in East Hampton, Long Island, New York. Her work includes: Plain Princess, McGinley, P. , Lippincott, 1945; Snow Is Falling, Branley, F. , Crowell, 1963.   ICB-1, ICB-2, ICB-3

STOVER, Jo Ann

She grew up on a farm near Peterborough, New Hampshire and attended the New England and Massachusetts Schools of Art. She married painter Paul Pollaro and has lived on Cape Cod and in New York City. Jo Ann Stover has been an art teacher, painter, illustrator, and author. Her work has been exhibited in many galleries. For boys and girls she illustrated: The Cheerful Quiet (A Junior Literary Guild selection), Horvath, B. , Watts, 1969; That Lucky Mrs Plucky, Evans, E. , McKay, 1961.

STUBIS, Talivaldis

He was born in Riga, Latvia and studied art at the University of Wisconsin. His work has appeared in the advertisements of the Broadway shows: "Camelot" and "Funny Girl". He also drew an advertisement for the movie "Night of the Iguana". He and his wife Patricia have lived in New York City. His work includes: A Pocketful of Seasons (A Junior Literary Guild selection), Foster, D. , Lothrop, 1961; Prove It!, Wyler, R. , Harper, 1963.

SUBA, Susanne   1913-

She was born in Budapest, Hungary, grew up in Europe
and the United States, and has lived in New York City.
She has also traveled and lived in Europe.   She received
her education in Brooklyn, New York at the Friends
School and Pratt Institute.   She was a recipient of a grant
for painting from the Michael Karolyi Memorial Foundation.   Miss Suba has received many awards for her work
in advertising including the Medal Award presented by the
Art Directors Club of Chicago.   Many of her books have
been listed in the American Institute of Graphic Arts
Fifty Books of the Year Exhibits, and her art work has
been exhibited in many museums.   For children she illustrated: A Flower From Dinah, Vance, M., Dutton, 1962;
Su An, Johnson, D., Follett, 1968. ICB-1, ICB-2, ICB-3

SWENEY, Frederic   1912-

He was born in Hollidaysburg, Pennsylvania and studied
at the Cleveland Institute of Art.   He has worked in advertising and also as an artist for the Cleveland Press.
He has taught art for a number of years at the Ringling
School of Art in Sarasota, Florida.   For young people
he illustrated Hawk In The Sky, Russell, F., Holt, 1965.

ICB-3

SZEKERES, Cyndy

She was born in Bridgeport, Connecticut and graduated
from Pratt Institute in Brooklyn, New York.   She married artist Gennaro Prozzo and has lived in Brooklyn
Heights.   She illustrated Jumper Goes To School, Parish,
P., Simon, 1969.

SZYK, Arthur 1894-1951

Born in Lodz, Poland, he studied art in Cracow and at
the Académie Julian and École des Beaux Arts in Paris.
In 1940 he came to the United States and became an
American citizen. His paintings on George Washington
hang in the Roosevelt Museum at Hyde Park, New York.
He has also illustrated for magazines including war cartoons which were published during World War II. He was
married to Julia Likerman and prior to his death lived
in Connecticut. He illustrated <u>Andersen's Fairy Tales,</u>
Lucas, E. (tr. by), Grosset, 1945.   ICB-2

TEE-VAN, Helen (Damrosch)

Artist, muralist, native New Yorker. She married Dr.
John Tee-Van, General Director of New York's Zoological Park and Aquarium. Her illustartions have appeared in scientific publications and in both <u>Collier's</u> and
<u>Britannica</u> Encyclopedias. Well-known for her illustra-
tions of animals, flowers, and undersea life, Mrs. Tee-
Van has served as artist on several expeditions with the
Tropical Research Department of the Zoological Society
of New York. In addition to painting murals for zoos
and museums, she has exhibited her work in New York
at the Museum of Natural History and the Metropolitan
Museum. For children she illustrated <u>Reptiles Round the
World</u>, Pope, C., Knopf, 1957. She also wrote and illustrated <u>Insects Are Where You Find Them</u>, Knopf, 1963.

TENGGREN, Gustaf 1896-

Artist and painter, born in Magra, Sweden. He came to
the United States in 1920 and has lived in West Southport,

Maine.   He received his education in Sweden at the Valand
School of Fine Arts in Gothenburg and the Slojdforeningens
School.   He has illustrated books for children both in this
country and in Scandinavia.   His work has been exhibited
abroad, and he has traveled and painted in Mexico, Nova
Scotia, and Yucatan.   His hobbies have included boating,
chess, and fishing.   Mr. Tenggren has received many
awards and honors for his book illustrations.   For children he illustrated: Pirates, Ships And Sailors, Jackson,
K. , Simon and Schuster, 1950; Tenggren's Cowboys And
Indians, Jackson, K. , Simon and Schuster, 1948.

                                                    ICB-1, ICB-2

TENNIEL, John   1820-1914

English cartoonist and illustrator, born in London.   For
nearly fifty years John Tenniel contributed political car-
toons to Punch.   He became well-known for his book il-
lustrations for children which include: Alice's Adventures
In Wonderland, Carroll, L. , Macmillan, 1865; Through
The Looking Glass And What Alice Saw There, Carroll,
L. , Macmillan, 1872.   (Mr. Tenniel has been listed in
"A Bibliography of Illustrators, " p. 441, ICB-1)

THOLLANDER, Earl Gustave   1922-

Artist, painter, born in Kingsburg, California, he grew
up in San Francisco.   He received his education at San
Francisco City College and the University of California
at Berkeley.   The artist also studied at the Art League
of California and at San Francisco's Art Institute and
Academy of Art.   He began his career in the advertising
field and also worked as a newspaper artist.   Mr. Thol-

lander has enjoyed travel and has made "drawing trips"
to Mexico, Europe, and the Orient.   His book illustrations include: Jump Frog Jump (A Junior Literary Guild
selection), Martin, P. , Putnam, 1965; To Catch A Mon-
goose, Ritchie, B. , Parnassus Press, 1963.   ICB-3

THOMAS, Glen
He was born in Sterling, Illinois.   He has always been
interested in railroads and has traveled on many types
of trains in various countries.   Mr. Thomas has specialized in all types of transportation in his work as an illustrator.   For young people he illustrated Giants Of the
Rails, Farrington, S. , Garden City, 1944.

THOMPSON, Mozelle
Artist and teacher, born in Pittsburgh, Pennsylvania.   He
attended the Carnegie Institute of Technology (now
Carnegie-Mellon University) and the Art Students League
in New York.   He also studied in Paris and New York on
a scholarship at the Parsons School of Design.   In addition to book illustration, Mr. Thompson has worked in
display and fashion design.   He has also been an instructor
at the Fashion Institute of Technology.   His book illustrations first appeared in Pumpkinseeds (A Junior Literary
Guild selection), Yezback, S. , Bobbs, 1969.

TOLFORD, Joshua 1909-
He was born in Thorp, Wisconsin and studied at the Lay-
ton School of Art in Milwaukee and the School of the
Museum of Fine Arts in Boston.   He also studied under
Anthony Thieme in Rockport, Massachusetts.   He and his

Tomes, Margot Ladd 1917-

artist wife have belonged to the Folly Cove Designers and
have made their home in Rockport. His work includes:
<u>Blitz</u>, Beatty, H., Houghton, 1961; <u>Trumper</u>, Beatty, H.,
Houghton, 1963; <u>Wicked John and the Devil</u>, Chase, R.,
Houghton, 1951.   ICB-2

TOMES, Margot Ladd 1917-
Artist, designer, born in Yonkers, New York. She studied
art at Pratt Institute in Brooklyn. Her cousins are
author-illustrator William Pène du Bois, designer Raoul
Pène du Bois, and painter Guy Pène du Bois. Her sister
Jacqueline has also illustrated children's books. In addition to book illustration, Margot Tomes has designed
fabrics, wallpaper, and book jackets. For young people
she illustrated: <u>In the Woods, In the Meadow, In the</u>
<u>Sky</u>, Fisher, A., Scribner, 1965; <u>Landslide!</u>, Day, V.
(tr. from the French by Margaret Morgan), Coward-Mc-
Cann, 1964.   ICB-3

TROYER, Johannes 1902-
Born in Austria (following World War I this particular
region became part of Italy), he studied there and in
Germany. He has been a calligrapher and illustrator for
American, Swiss, and German publishers. He designed
several postage stamps for the principality of Liechten-
stein and has also designed type faces. Mr. Troyer came
to the United States in 1949 and lived in New Rochelle,
New York. He returned to Europe to make his home in
1961. His work includes: <u>Baby Jesus</u>, Mason, M.,
Macmillan, 1959; <u>The Golden Lynx And Other Tales</u>,
Baker, A., Lippincott, 1960.   ICB-2, ICB-3

TRUMBULL, John   1756-1843

Artist, painter, born in Lebanon, Connecticut. He at-
tended Harvard University and also studied in London.
A noted American painter of the early nineteenth century,
four of his murals hang in the Capitol Rotunda in Wash-
ington, D. C. His portraits have included: Washington,
Jefferson, and Adams. His paintings also hang in the
Art Gallery at Yale University. His work appeared in
With Colors Flying, Buranelli, M. , Crowell, 1969.

TURKLE, Brinton Cassaday   1915-

Artist, designer, writer, born in Alliance, Ohio. He
studied at Carnegie Institute of Technology in Pittsburgh,
Pennsylvania before attending art school in Boston. After
further study at Chicago's Institute of Design, Mr. Turkle
began his career in book illustration in Santa Fe, New
Mexico. He later made his home in New York City. His
main interest has been the theater, and he has been both
an actor and director. He has worked in advertising,
and his theatrical caricatures have appeared in newspapers. He has also been the author of several children's books. Juvenile books which he wrote and illustrated include: The Magic of Millicent Musgrave (A
Junior Literary Guild selection), Viking 1967; Obadiah
the Bold, Viking, 1965. He also illustrated Indian
Children of America, Farquhar, M. , Holt, 1964. ICB-3

VALLI   see   VAN DE BOVENCAMP, Valli

VAN DE BOVENCAMP, Valli

Illustrator and designer, born in Bucharest, Romania.

She has used Valli as her professional name. She came
to the United States as a child and later made her home
in New York City where she has been associated with
NBC as a free-lance designer of animation and promotional
films. Miss Van de Bovencamp received her education
at Finch College and Columbia and Michigan Universities.
She also studied in Geneva and Paris. She illustrated
Talking Leaves (A Junior Literary Guild selection), Kohn,
B., Hawthorn, 1969.

VASILIU, Mircea 1920-

He was born in Bucharest, Rumania and recieved a law
degree from the University of Bucharest. He later studied
art at the Corcoran School of Art in Washington, D. C.
and the Art Students League in New York. He had his
first book published at the age of thirteen. Mircea Vasiliu has written and illustrated books for both children and
adults. He and his wife have lived in Riverdale, New
York. His work includes: The Story Of Numbers, Lauber,
P., Random, 1961; Miss Agatha's Lark, Sherman, N.,
Bobbs, 1968.   ICB-2, ICB-3

VAUGHAN-JACKSON, Genevieve 1913-

Born in England, she spent part of her childhood in Ireland and studied in France at the Sorbonne, Atelier Ar-
mand-Delille, Ville d'Avray, Seine et Oise, and at the
Central School of Arts and Crafts in London. She came
to the United States in 1937. Married to geologist John
A. Shimer, she has lived in New York City. She illustrated The North American Wolf, Venn, M., Hastings
House, 1965 and was the author of Carramore, Hastings,
1968.   ICB-2

VICTOR, Joan Berg 1937-

Born in Chicago, she graduated from Tulane University
in New Orleans and received her master's degree from
Yale University.   Her drawings and paintings have appeared in many galleries throughout America.   She also
had a one-woman-show in New York City where she has
made her home.   Her work includes: Aunt America,
Bloch, M., Atheneum, 1963; The First Christmas Gifts,
Pauli, H., Washburn, 1965.   ICB-3

VOSBURGH, Leonard

He was born in Yonkers, New York, went to school in
North Plainfield, New Jersey, and spent summer vacations
in the Mohawk Valley of New York.   He studied art at
Pratt Institute and the Art Students League in New York.
Prior to illustrating books, he worked in advertising.
His water colors have been exhibited at the National Acad-
emy and the American Water Color Society.   His work
includes: Crown Point, the Destiny Road, Wilson, C.,
McKay, 1965; Fear In the Forest, DeLeeuw, C., Nelson,
1960; Gateway to America, Pauli, H., McKay, 1965.

WADOWSKI-BAK, Alice

Artist-teacher, born in New York near Buffalo.   She received degrees from Syracuse and Buffalo Universities.
She has been an art instructor at New York City's Academy of the Sacred Heart.   In addition to book illustration,
her work has also appeared in such magazines as Jubilee
and Woman's Day.   For children she illustrated Encounter
Near Venus, Wibberley, L., Farrar, 1967.

WALKER, Charles W.

He was born in Hempstead, Long Island and later made his home in Yorktown Heights, New York. He studied art at Syracuse University's College of Fine Arts. In addition to book illustration, the artist has also worked in advertising. For boys and girls he illustrated White Water, Still Water, Bosworth, J., Doubleday, 1966.

WALKER, Nedda

Born in Canada, her childhood was spent in Boston. She studied art at the Pennsylvania Academy in Philadelphia and also studied privately in Europe. In addition to illustrating books for boys and girls, she has been a portrait painter. Her work includes: In The Beginning, Trent, R., Westminster Press, 1949.   ICB-2

WALTERS, Audrey

Artist and cartoonist, born in Philadelphia, Pennsylvania. Her summer home (a Victorian cottage) on Cape May provided the background for many of her drawings. In addition to books, Mrs. Walters has done magazine illustrations. She has also created animated cartoons. For children she illustrated Just Like You...., Klein, L., Harvey House, 1968.

WALTRIP, Mildred 1911-

She was born in Kentucky and studied art at the Chicago Art Institute. Following graduation, she traveled and studied in Europe for a year on a fellowship. She has done free-lance work in New York and Chicago. Mildred Waltrip has created displays for stores and painted murals

in addition to her book illustrations which include First
Book Of Water, Smith, F. , Watts, 1959.

WARD, Lynd Kendall 1905-

Artist, author. He married writer May McNeer whom
he met while attending Columbia University. When they
were first married, they lived in Leipzig where Mr. Ward
studied graphic arts. He has written many books with
his wife, and he has been an outstanding illustrator. Mr.
Ward has been equally proficient in water color, lithog-
raphy, and oil. They have lived in Leonia, New Jersey.
He illustrated May McNeer's The American Indian Story,
Ariel Bks. , 1963 and Esther Forbes' America's Paul Revere, Houghton, 1946. He was awarded the Caldecott
Medal in 1953 for his book. The Biggest Bear, Houghton,
1952. (Authors Of Books For Young People-1964)

ICB-1, ICB-2, ICB-3

WATSON, Aldren Auld 1917-

Born in Brooklyn, New York, he received his early education in Quaker schools and later attended Yale University in New Haven, Connecticut and the Art Students League
in New York. His interests have included cartography
and bookbinding. He has also been a map draftsman for
textbooks and Time magazine. After World War II, in
which he and his wife served as field workers for the
American Friends Service Committee, the artist made his
home in Putney, Vermont. Aldren Watson has illustrated
many of his wife's books. His drawings can also be
found in Prehistoric America, White, A. , Random, 1951.

ICB-1, ICB-2, ICB-3

WATSON, Howard N.

Artist and teacher.   His home has been in Germantown,
Pennsylvania.   Mr. Watson has been on the staff at the
Philadelphia College of Art.   His work has often been
exhibited at art galleries in the East.   For boys and
girls he illustrated Garbage Can Cat, Sharoff, V., Westminster, 1969.

WATSON, Wendy

She was born in Putney, Vermont, the daughter of artist
Aldren Watson.   She graduated from Bryn Mawr College
in Pennsylvania.   In addition to the books which she has
illustrated for children, Wendy Watson has also been the
author of several juvenile stories.   Her work includes:
The Spider Plant, Speevack, Y., Atheneum, 1965; When
Noodlehead Went to the Fair, Hitte, K., Parents', 1968.

WEGNER, Fritz   1924-

Born in Vienna, Austria, he studied at St. Martin's
School of Art in London.   He later taught graphic design
at St. Martin's.   Mr. Wegner's drawings have often appeared in British publications.   His home has been in
Highgate, North London.   For boys and girls he illustrated Fattypuffs & Thinifers (First American Edition),
Maurois, A., Knopf, 1968.   ICB-2

WEIL, Lisl

She was born in Vienna, Austria and studied at Wiener
Kunstgewerbeschule.   Prior to coming to the United
States in 1939, she worked on a Viennese newspaper and
magazine.   She has conducted a weekly television show

("Children's Sketch Book") and drawn pictures to music
on the concert stage (Little Orchestra Society's children's
concerts at Lincoln Center).   She and her husband have
lived in New York City.   She wrote and illustrated:
Bitzli and the Big Bad Wolf, Houghton, 1960; Eyes So-o
Big, Houghton, 1964; Mimi, Houghton, 1961.

ICB-2, ICB-3

WEINHEIMER, George

His home has been in Schenectady, New York.   In addition to his work as an illustrator of children's books,
Mr. Weinheimer has been principal of an elementary
school.   He has also conducted a children's art program
over educational television.   The Weinheimer household
has included four children plus a large assortment of
pets.   For boys and girls he illustrated The Dreaming
Zoo, Unterecker, J., Walck, 1965.

WEISGARD, Leonard 1916-

Born in New Haven, Connecticut, this illustrator-author
attended Pratt Institute.   He has worked on magazines
and designed sets for the ballet.   Mr. Weisgard has
lived in Danbury and Roxbury, Connecticut.   Numerous
authors have had their books illustrated by him.   His
illustrations in The Little Island (written by Margaret
Wise Brown, Doubleday, 1946) won the 1947 Caldecott
Medal.   His books include: Mr. Peaceable Paints,
Scribner, 1956; Pelican Here, Pelican There, Scribner,
1948; Silly Willy Nilly, Scribner, 1953.   (Authors Of
Books For Young People-1964)   ICB-1, ICB-2, ICB-3

WEISS, Emil 1896-1965

Illustrator, newspaper artist, designer. Born in Olmutz, Moravia, Austria, he later lived in England and New York City where he died in 1965. He received a degree in architecture from Austria's University of Vienna. Emil Weiss was a war artist during World War I. He later became well-known for his sketches which appeared in newspapers in Prague, Czechoslovakia and London, England. He also designed costumes and film sets. After service with the British Army during World War II, Mr. Weiss was commissioned by the Royal Engineers Hall of Fame to sketch various Generals of the British Army. He has also served as a press artist to the United Nations. For children he illustrated: Papa Luigi's Marionettes, Paul, L., Washburn, 1962; Seeing Fingers (A Junior Literary Guild selection), De Gering, E., McKay, 1962.   ICB-3

WENNERSTROM, Genia Katherine 1930-
Her pseudonym is Genia. Born in New York City, she attended the New School for Social Research and New York University. She also studied at Pratt Institute in Brooklyn. She married an artist and has lived in Forest Hills. In addition to books, she has illustrated greeting cards, magazines, and fashions. She also designed a ninety-foot sign for a mountain top in New Jersey. For children she illustrated Tekla's Easter, Budd, L., Rand, 1962.   ICB-3

WERTH, Kurt 1896-
Born in Leipzig, Germany, Mr. Werth received his ed-

ucation at Leipzig's Academy for Graphic Arts.   He began his career in book illustration in Munich.   German
magazines also published his drawings.   When the Hitler
regime came into power, the Werth family came to the
United States.   He became an American citizen and has
lived in Riverdale, New York.   For young people he illustrated: Herbert's Space Trip, Wilson, H., Knopf, 1965;
Isabelle and the Library Cat, Bason, L., Lothrop, 1966;
A Tiger Called Thomas (A Junior Literary Guild selection), Zolotow, C., Lothrop, 1963.   ICB-2, ICB-3

WHITE, David Omar

He studied in California at the Claremont Graduate School
under Henry Lee McFee.   He has done satiric drawings
in addition to his book illustrations.   His own children
have provided inspiration for several of his picture books.
For young people he illustrated Sophia Scrooby Preserved,
Bacon, M., Little, 1968.

WIESNER, William   1899-

He graduated from the University of Vienna with degrees
in engineering and architecture.   He has been an interior
decorator, architect, and designer.   He also once operated a shadow-puppet theater.   He and his wife have
worked in textile design, and their work was in the Metropolitan Museum's 1945 exhibit entitled "American Fabrics and Fashions."   The Wiesners have lived in New
York City.   He illustrated Hobnob (A Junior Literary
Guild selection), Wilson, C., Viking, 1968.

                                            ICB-2, ICB-3

WILDSMITH, Brian Lawrence 1930-

He was born in Penistone, Yorkshire, England, grew up
in Sheffield, and studied at the Barnsley School of Art,
London's Slade School of Fine Art, and University College
in London.   Prior to doing free-lance work, he was an
art teacher.   He was awarded the 1962 Kate Greenaway
Medal for his ABC, Watts, 1962.   His other books include: Brian Wildsmith's Birds, Watts, 1967; Brian Wildsmith's Fishes, Watts, 1968; Brian Wildsmith's 1, 2,
3's, Watts, 1965; Wild Animals, Watts, 1967.   ICB-3

WILKIN, Eloise Burns 1904-

Born in Rochester, New York, she grew up there and in
New York City.   She studied at Rochester Institute of
Technology.   Following school, she went to New York
City where she began her career in book illustration.
She has lived in Canandaigua, New York.   For boys and
girls she illustrated: Seatmates, Reely, M., Watts,
1949; Tune Is In The Tree, Lovelace, M., Crowell, 1950.

                                    ICB-1, ICB-2

WILKON, Jozef 1930-

The son of an artist, he was born near Cracow, Poland.
He grew up in Wieliczka and studied in Cracow at Jag-
iellonski University and the Academy of Art.   His home
has been in Warsaw, Poland.   His book illustrations have
been published by Polish, German, and French publishers.
Jozef Wilkon has been the recipient of many awards including both the 1960 and 1962 Polish Editors' Award for
the "Most Beautiful Book of the Year."   He also won the
"Most Beautiful" German book award in 1965.   For young

readers he illustrated <u>The Crane With One Leg</u>, Schaaf, P., Warne, 1964.

WILLCOX, Sandra

She spent her childhood in St. Paul and later studied at the University of Minnesota. Prior to teaching art in schools of the Caledonia-Orange Supervisory School District in Newbury, Vermont, Mrs. Willcox taught art at Peacham Academy in Peacham, Vermont. Her husband has been a writer and sculptor, and they have lived in Peacham. For young people she illustrated <u>Ditto</u> (A Junior Literary Guild selection), Clayton, B., Funk, 1968.

WILSON, John

Born in Houston, he graduated from Boston's School of the Museum of Fine Arts and received a B. S. in Education from Tufts University in Medford, Massachusetts. Mr. Wilson has been honored with many awards. His work has been exhibited in the United States and Jerusalem and can be found in private collections. For boys and girls he illustrated: <u>Spring Comes to the Ocean</u>, George, J., Crowell, 1966; <u>Striped Ice Cream</u>, Lexau, J., Lippincott, 1968.

WONG, Jeanyee 1920-

Artist, illustrator, painter. Born in San Francisco, California, she later made her home in New York City. Jeanyee Wong received her art training at New York's Cooper Union School of Art. She also had private study in illustration and woodcutting. She has worked in cal-

ligraphy, design, and sculpture in addition to book illustration.   For young readers she illustrated The Story Of
India, Bothwell, J., Harcourt, 1952.   ICB-2

WYETH, Newell Convers 1882-1945
Artist-muralist.   He was born in Needham, Massachusetts
and studied with artist Howard Pyle.   At one time he
lived in Colorado and New Mexico.   He encouraged his
son Andrew to learn to paint and draw.   For boys and
girls he illustrated: The Deerslayer, Cooper, J., Scribner's 1925; The Little Shepherd Of Kingdom Come, Scribner's, 1931; Robin Hood, Creswick, P., McKay, 1917.

YAMAGUCHI, Marianne Illenberger 1936-
Born in Cuyahoga Falls, Ohio, she studied at Bowling
Green State University and the Rhode Island School of Design.   She married Tohr Yamaguchi, and they have lived
and studied in Australia.   She illustrated her husband's
books: ... The Golden Crane, Holt, 1963; Two Crabs In
The Moonlight, Holt, 1965.   ICB-3

YAP, Weda 1894-
Born Louise Drew Cook in Philadelphia, Pennsylvania,
she grew up there and in Bar Harbor, Maine.   She
studied at the Museum School of Industrial Art in Philadelphia, New York's Art Students League, and the Win-
old Riess Art School.   Mrs. Yap received private in-
struction in the graphic arts and portrait painting.   She
also studied abroad in Italy, France, and Germany.   At
one time the artist traveled and lived in China and other
countries of the Far East.   She worked as a marine

draftsman during World War II.   Her home has been in
Morristown, New Jersey.   For children she illustrated:
Junior Science Book of Rain, Hail, Sleet & Snow, Lar-
rick, N. , Garrard, 1961; Junior Science Book of Weather
Experiments, Feravolo, R. , Garrard, 1963.   ICB-2

YOUNG, Ed
Artist, illustrator, teacher, born in Shanghai, China.   He
has been on the staff of Pratt Institute where he has
taught visual communication.   In 1968 a book which he
illustrated The Emperor And The Kite (Yolen, J. , World,
1967) was designated a runner-up for the Caldecott Medal.
He and his wife, a ceramist, have lived in New York
City.   His work includes: Chinese Mother Goose Rhymes,
Wyndham, R. , ed. , World, 1968; The Mean Mouse, And
Other Mean Stories, Udry, J. , Harper, 1962.

ZALLINGER: Jean Day   1918-
She was born in Boston, grew up in Braintree, Massachusetts, and graduated from the Massachusetts College
of Art and the Yale School of Fine Arts.   She married
artist Rudolph Zallinger, and they have lived in Connecticut.   In addition to illustrating books for young people
and the Wildlife Federation, her work has appeared in
Collier's Encyclopedia.   For young people she illustrated:
In the Days Of The Dinosaurs, Andrews, R. , Random,
1959; Junior Science Book Of Pond Life, Crosby, A. ,
Garrard, 1964.   ICB-3

ZEMACH, Margot   1931-
She was born in Los Angeles, California, grew up in

New York City, and attended the County Art Institute in Los Angeles. She also studied at the Jepson and Kann Art Institutes and was awarded a Fulbright Scholarship to study in Vienna, Austria in 1955-56. She married history professor and writer Harve Zemach, and they have lived in Newton Centre, Massachusetts. She illustrated the Prize picture book Salt (adapted by Harve Zemach, Follett, 1965) in the 1965 Book Week's Spring Book Festival. Other juvenile books which she illustrated include: Harlequin, Mincieli, R., Knopf, 1968; The Question Box, Williams, J., Norton, 1965.   ICB-3

Caldecott Medal Winners

1970 Sylvester And The Magic Pebble, Steig, 118

1969 The Fool Of The World And The Flying Ship,
Shulevitz, 112

1968 Drummer Hoff, Emberley, 35

1967 Sam, Bangs, & Moonshine, Ness, 88

1966 Always Room For One More, Hogrogian, 52

1965 May I Bring A Friend?, Montresor, 83

1964 Where The Wild Things Are, Sendak, 108

1963 The Snowy Day, Keats, 59

1962 Once A Mouse, Brown, 20

1961 Baboushka And The Three Kings, Sidjakov, 113

1960 Nine Days To Christmas, Ets, 36

1959 Chanticleer And The Fox, Cooney, 26-27

1958 Time Of Wonder, McCloskey, 72

1957 A Tree Is Nice, Simont, 114

1956 Frog Went A-Courtin', Rojankovsky, 102

1955 Cinderella, Brown, 20

1954 Madeline's Rescue, Bemelmans, 12

1953 The Biggest Bear, Ward, 131

1952 Finders Keepers, Mordvinoff, 84

1951 The Egg Tree, Milhous, 81

1950 Song Of The Swallows, Politi, 94

1949 The Big Snow, Hader, 49

1948 White Snow, Bright Snow, Duvoisin, 33

1947 The Little Island, Weisgard, 133

1946 The Rooster Crows, Petersham, 92

Title Index

Note: Name following title is illustrator's; number
refers to page

A For The Ark, Duvoisin, 33
ABC, Wildsmith, 136
Abe Lincoln Gets His Chance, Hutchison, 54
Abraham Lincoln, D'Aulaire, 30
Abraham Lincoln: Man Of Courage, Goldstein, 44
Achilles The Donkey, Barker, 10
Action At Paradise Marsh, Blust, 15
Adlai Stevenson: Young Ambassador, Goldstein, 44
Adventure Of Walter, Fetz, 38
Adventures And Discoveries Of Marco Polo, Baldridge, 10
Adventures Of Arab, Slobodkin, 115
Adventures Of Huckleberry Finn, Rockwell, 101
Adventures Of Tom Leigh, Silverman, 113-114
Algernon And The Pigeons, Mizumura, 83
Alice's Adventures In Wonderland, Tenniel, 124
All About Biology, Cellini, 24
All About Eggs, Ludwig, 71
All About The Weather, Martin, 78
All Except Sammy, Shimin, 110
All In Free But Janey, Hyman, 54
All The Silver Pennies, Arndt, 8
Always Room For One More, Hogrogian, 52
American ABC, Petersham, 92

143

144

146

158

DATE DUE